HIS EYE IS ON THE SPARROW SO...

This Is Really for the Birds

HIS EYE IS ON THE SPARROW SO...

This Is Really for the Birds

Charlene Potterbaum

Logos International
Plainfield, New Jersey

Grateful acknowledgment is made for material taken from the following books:

Under His Wings by O. Hallesby. Published by Augsburg Publishing House. Copyright © 1932, 1960, pp. 146-147.

To Kiss the Joy by Robert A. Raines. Published by Word Books of Waco, Texas. Copyright © 1973, pp. 71-72.

Dedicated to . . .

The warm little flock that bears our resemblance. . . . To Don, Janis and Laurie, who have already tumbled from the nest and made some of their own.

To Larry, who is still somewhat poised in flight . . . and to Mark and Jamie who have nearly outgrown the prickly premises we share together as they soar toward manhood on their way through puberty.

But most of all I dedicate this to my hard-working husband, Gene, who is, after thirty years of marriage, still willing to snuggle with me *in* the nest, in spite of the fact that my feathers droop and sag a bit, and that I peck at him occasionally.

Preface

I know it's a silly title, but if you have purchased this book, leafed through it a bit and even bothered to read it this far, then it might not have been such a bad idea after all.

You see, publishers seem to like my books, but seldom appreciate my knack for titles. When I told Vi Malachuk about my original choice, she rolled her eyes, clutched her turtleneck (sweater, I mean) and sighed "O-o-oh, but my dear, *Seven Cedar Waxwings* will never do. I mean, that's *really* for the birds!"

Which only goes to show you how green, how naive, how unprofessional I am when it comes to the fascinating business of attracting. Readers, that is.

But I do have a great thing going for me. You see, *Jesus loves me!* And when I do what I do as "unto Him," He, for His own sweet reasons, chooses to bless that endeavor! There is just no blessing that can be compared with working cooperatively with the Creator of the universe, the Savior of the world.

So this is our labor of love—His and mine. He and I have wept over it, laughed about it, blue-penciled in love together throughout it. And please accept my apology, as I know it must smack of "me" in many instances. But when all my works are burned up, I pray that there might be some little gem left—some precious jewel that I can lay at His feet. But in the meantime, I thank you for your willingness to poke through all the hay and stubble to get to the pearl of great price He holds out to you.

HIS EYE IS ON THE SPARROW SO...

This Is Really
for the Birds

1

I'd just stepped into the family room, my arms piled high with delinquent laundry, when I saw them. Seven, little, delicately featured bandits were stashing loot into their beaks from the berry bush outside my picture window with complete abandon and what appeared to be a rather ravenous neurotic urgency.

I don't know when I've seen a sight so breathtaking. Granted, it could have been the dash up from the laundry room, but I preferred to think my palpitations were due to my aesthetic nature.

I really drank it all in . . . little black masks, a mousy, mauve softness, tails threaded with a strip of yellow rainbow, a saucy tufted topknot and great community spirit.

It was obvious that they were prone to gluttony, so I felt they'd be staying around long enough to be identified. I dumped the laundry unceremoniously onto the couch and went for my bird book. I mean, being biologically enriched beats sorting clothes all to pieces! My family always went nearly into hysterics when they'd see me clutching my bird book. They'd tease my husband, Gene, informing him that his long trips out of town were affecting me . . . ah, yes. Page 103—cedar waxwings. Hm-m-m. Said to be mysterious birds. Well, my soft, mundane world of pancake batter and bedroom clutter doesn't really turn the average teenager on. Or the worldly wise predominant breadwinner, either, for that matter. Maybe mysterious birds would do the trick.

Well, I really felt I could dramatize this with great appeal and hold the interest of my family for at least, say . . . thirty seconds. Even went so far as to rehearse it in my mind several times, with page 103 open for quick reference. Goodness, maybe the Audubon Society would invite me to speak, I fantasized—

By ones and twos, they came in. My children, I mean. Not the birds . . . although I must confess that for a fleeting moment I wanted to open the door just to see if maybe I didn't have some of that same "animal magnetism" that St. Francis of Assisi had. I waited until the din of cookie-jar slamming, refrigerator-door flapping and candy-wrapper crackling had subsided before I blandly mentioned, "Mark, you should have seen the delicious sight I . . . ."

"Oh, mom! Glad you said delicious . . . almost forgot to tell you that I volunteered you to make candy for school . . . but nothin' gooey, mom. Too many braces, y'know," as he flashed his own wire-encased-dental-retirement-payment-plan grin my way.

"And mom, can't talk now . . . gotta' get some dry ice and dynamite fuses for some experiments! Bye, now—and, oh yeah, mom . . . I need my gym shorts for tomorrow."

Nonplused, I turned to Laurie. "Honey, this morning, just out there on the berry bush, I—"

"Mom! Speaking of bush, I just remembered I'd promised Stacy I'd come and put straightener on her hair. Can I take the car? Thanks, mom."

Mom? Might as well be "memo." But I did my best to see

where straightener and dynamite fuses would take precedence over soft, gentle, feathered things. (*Dynamite fuses! Must remember to ask him where these experiments were taking place. . . .*)

Well, it's all right. Gene would be interested. He was a good husband, and he would care about my day. But as I put page 103 back into the bird book drawer, I somehow wished I felt a bit less like the distraught housewife of *Come Back, Little Sheba.*

That evening, Gene came in, planted a warm kiss on my cheek, and himself in his easy chair. By now, creamed broccoli and a crackling newspaper had pushed any memory of feathery invaders out of my mind. Besides, this was the ominous time of the day when, by some mysterious osmosis, Gene and the evening newspaper became one and the same. Any attempt at communication would only result in a low guttural response, accompanied by a flip of the sports page, or maybe a quote from the classifieds.

And so, during dinner, I found myself gingerly wedging my way through a maze of football scores and what latest car really had pizazz, to finally finagle a timid "I don't know if anyone would be interested or not, but today. . . ."

Gene interrupted. " 'Scuse me, hon. Larry, would you please pass the gravy."

"Sure, dad. One lump or two?" Of course the round of giggles complete with choking emphasis and spluttering guffaws soon eased the conversation back into the old time-worn but comfortable niche of sports plays, science experiments and Laurie's love life.

And Gene, recalling I'd started to say something, encouraged me to go on, but I just laughingly shook my head and groaned, "What I had to say would come on like a slug of castor oil after that gravy morsel—you can wait and read it in

3

my next book. It'll keep."

And really, it didn't matter. I felt a sweet Presence around that happy table, and was learning a valuable lesson. I was discovering that because God *is* a personal God, some of life's precious moments were exactly that—*personal*. Just meant for God and me, alone. And as much as I loved this crazy, rollicking bunch He'd given me, I wasn't quite sure they were ready for my little cedar waxwings . . . *seven* cedar waxwings. Hm-m-m-m. *Seven Cedar Waxwings*. Who knows? Might even make a good book title, someday.

2

Kisses, hugs, doors slamming, cars starting, gym bags bumping, last-minute checks for lunch tickets, field trip slips, baseball mitts, briefcases . . . one by one they stand before me, as before a tribunal. "Mom, does my hair look all right?" . . . "Do I look dumb in this?" . . . "Mom, does this make me look fat?" . . . "Be here when I get home, okay, mom?" as they leave the trauma center here at 1440 to seek the warmth and security of their particular peer groups that make the cold, impersonal world a habitable place for them to grow in.

And me? Quietly, after the noisy exodus, I admit to myself that I've just made it with flying colors through one of the day's most trying hours as I slip into my favorite mulling-over place, tuck my inexpensive robe around my too expansive body while sipping very expensive coffee from an un-exquisite mug. For just a few treasured and blessed moments I listen to the dust settle, pipes wheeze, fluorescents choke and splutter, veritably drinking in the stillness, and loving it. (If you've never heard the dust settle at your house, it's only because you've never raised six children. Here, at 1440, it plummets earthward like meteors.)

In these moments of bliss I give my offerings of praise to Him, or hormonally speaking, my *sacrifice* of praise, depending on what part of the monthly cycle I happen to be tiptoing through at the time.

You see, for three weeks out of the month, I can genuinely thank and praise Him for my "calling"—that of wife and mother. I truly love my feminine role and praise Him for our home complete with cobwebs, crabgrass and shower fungus. For three weeks, that is. For one week, I hold on to His hand for dear life, thanking Him, not so much because I feel like it, but because He told me to! Whether *I feel like it or not!* But this week of the cycle is usually the most rewarding, spiritually, because I learn to respond to Him in deliberate obedience, rather than siding with my unreliable emotions that would encourage me to whimper.

Well, regardless of which part of the cycle I'm in, I make an effort to "re-cycle" all my thoughts by bringing them captive and compliant to the obedience of Christ. The Mary heart of me lovingly bows before Him as time and eternity blend together into one all resplendent NOW.

But then slowly, and I must add, somewhat reluctantly, the Martha part of me begins to chide, and I know I must, by an act of my will, turn from that place of warmth and reality there at His feet, to the harshness and quasi-reality around me. I must, again, by an act of my will turn from the books that beckon so invitingly to me; from the typewriter with all its great creative reserve . . . and turn, again, by a deliberate act of my will, to the dusting (yes, one could say I was definitely a woman of the "cloth") and to the solid realization that love "covers a multitude of sins" . . . and picks up an awful lot of junk.

God reveals His plan for me, gently, via the telephone, the doorbell, household chores, demands of others. And what's it all about? It's just being God's representative in the midst of daily living. It's just being about His business by minding my own assigned busy-ness. It's His presence anointing the ordinariness of life, causing it to blossom into the extraordinariness of abundant life. Learning to be aware of His Presence, not so much in the milling crowd, but in the sweetness of solitude . . .while wiping a counter top, scraping a broiler, scrubbing a stool, folding a sheet, cleaning a carrot, doubling a recipe, refinishing furniture, wallpapering, painting . . . He is there, to assist, to comfort, remind, grant patience, give confidence, to cheer, and to lend companionship.

In short, it is a nestling down into one of the tender maxims of Christianity, for someone much wiser than I stated that "the chief end of man is to glorify God and enjoy Him forever." There is only one way to enjoy Him forever—by learning to adore Him in the relentless NOW . . . for this moment . . . and the next . . . and the turbulent next . . . the sum total of all our moments being . . . forever!

3

Phooey! The garage was blocked by several teenagers' cars. I beeped for help, got out of the car, managing to slam my finger in the car door as Mark, my fourteen-year-old, bounded out of the house to carry in the groceries. I moved aside, giving him a wide berth to the trunk, and unwittingly stepped into a bank of wet slush. A throbbing hand, iced foot and pain-inflicted nausea were doing nothing to discourage the surly feelings already engulfing me. Now, with the discovery that my house must surely be crawling with teenagers, I wondered if maybe a term on the mission field wouldn't have been easier. . . .

Mark didn't notice my foul mood. As he swung by me toward the porch, arms laden with groceries—very expensive groceries, I might add—he quipped, "Hey, mom, the pastor where you'll be speaking next week, he called, wanted to know if you had a favorite number they could use for the music part of the program. . . ."

"How thoughtful," I commented as I watched my glowing finger. "What did you tell him?"

"Nothin' "—impish grin—"I just hummed a few bars of 'You dee-serve a break to-da-a-ay—at McDon . . . .' "

"You *didn't!*" and just that quickly my negative feeling

8

lifted as we laughed together. Truly, a merry heart doeth good like a medicine. I rumpled his hair, sent him back to his friends and began putting the groceries away.

A part of my mind was trying to figure out what might have caused me to entertain such negative thoughts and another part of my mind was realistically sizing up the condition of the inside of the refrigerator. Sandblasting would have been the simplest solution, but the second best "solution" was baking soda water, and while sloshing around in it, I wondered if I oughtn't to drink some of it, as both interiors obviously needed some attention.

"No," whispered the Minister of my Interior—the Holy Spirit. "That won't be necessary. Just bring your problems to me, and I will do the cleansing."

And so, one by one, I brought my problems to Him as I scraped off gooey residue and gouged stubborn deposits loose. There, just to the left of my heart, was a blob of ingratitude. In an unguarded moment, I'd taken my eyes off of Jesus and zeroed in on my circumstances. I'd become obsessed by the things that weren't working smoothly—the broken water softener, the leaking faucet, the dryer-that-wouldn't-dry, the garage door opener I couldn't find . . . and, Gene was out of town.

And there, hanging on a hinge, was a gob of impatience! I wanted that dryer fixed, and I wanted it *right now!* And to the right of my malfunctioning forgiver lodged a glob of discouragement. And here on the bottom rack, breaking the fingernail on my right thumb, is self-loathing! (Scratch, scrape, gouge.) Away with you! I wiped up ingratitude by beginning to thank God because He was greater than any of my problems, gentler than any of my rudenesses, and was willing to exchange my weakness for His strength at any "called upon" moment.

9

I did away with self-loathing by forgiving myself for being
. . . yes, less than perfect!

I realized, as I wrung out the now somewhat slimy rag, that
the need to forgive myself of imperfections was *just* as
necessary as forgiving my neighbor . . . that, although I
detested some of the (*all* of the) stupid things I do, I had no
right to detest *myself,* for, wonder of wonders, I was made in
His likeness, and if He felt I was worth dying for, surely I could
feel I am worth living *with!*

I removed myself from inside the refrigerator with a grunt
and a giggle, closed the door gently and thought of what a
strange place I'd chosen for a prayer closet. But I knew that
God could now inspect both interiors and find them
gleaming.

4

Mark doesn't know it, but he is outside building strong character. He is sousing the car immaculate. When he came in the house for more towels, I said, "Honey, you must really enjoy car-washing. No one asked you to do it, and you're taking such pains. . . ."

He slugged down a cold drink, wiped his forehead on my best kitchen towel—the one I'd intended to dry dishes with—and said, "Actually, mom, I *hate* it! But it needed it, and as long as I'm doing it, might's well do it right. . . ." And off he went into the sun, swathed in chamois and sponges.

And me? I fell into the nearest chair. Few mothers could stand the shock that comes with discovering that yes, somewhere along the line, the desperate, agonizing, nagging, frustrating line of if-you-have-to-do-something-you-might-as-well-do-it-right, the words have sunk in somewhere and taken root in the heart as a proper attitude. (Somewhere, I'd seen a quote that said, "Why is there never enough time to do it right, but always enough time to do it over?")

And later, when I heard him clattering and banging the sweeper into its allotted niche, I felt an even warmer glow . . . the putting-away-of-things had also been an oft-repeated refrain down through the years. But after the

11

warm glow, then the maternal ache. Mark was growing up—so soon, so soon—and with a strong character and a knowledge of God. Could I ask for anything more?

5

I have two perfect children in my home. They never sass, never lose things, never grumble, never tattle, outgrow their clothes, wear out shoes, need doctors, or dentists. They always stay within their boundaries . . . which happen to be a pair of maple frames nailed securely to my kitchen wall!

The *real* ones I've raised, and am raising, embarrass me in public, threaten my sanity, provoke me both to love and anger . . . melt my heart, grieve my spirit, splinter my nerve ends, engender compassion, ruin my furniture, and cause my heart to alternately burst with pride and fury, mingled with an oft-expressed desire to lock them in a closet for at least a season, depending on which stage of growth they are in.

And as you might have guessed, with six children living in our domain, I wasn't the only one who felt this way. Neighbors often voiced similar sentiments. We even had a cuckoo clock that would only "cuckoo" between the hours of two and four, when the children were napping. I think Jamie's crouching behind sofas with his Davy Crockett musket had something to do with that. Jamie is my youngest, most rambunctious son.

Any move into a new neighborhood had to be executed after dark. What with six kids, a drum set, cornet, two motorcycles and a neurotic puppy, one can't be too careful.

I guess I had some glossy, unstable notion that once children were married, you'd be free of the deep concern that constricts every mother's heart . . . but not so. The training period may be over, but then the time comes when God must gently box them on their ears, test their faith, and engineer their circumstances, just as He did for you. Then you must sit back, feel grave concern and groan inwardly as you see them making wrong decisions. I'm talking of grave concern in terms of "God have mercy on them as they take this longer route to you" and not in terms of useless worry that says "it will never work—there is no hope."

Once, when I saw one of them turning to his own willful way instead of towards God's restful, refreshing way, I wept before the Lord for this, my wayward child. I felt at that moment what so many mothers have felt . . . that it was my fault, that I'd tried so hard . . . and my heart's cry was, "God, I love you so much . . . my deepest heart's desire is for them to love you, and bring glory to you . . . how can it be, when I love you with every part of me, that they have not turned to you?"

So comfortingly, He wiped the tears from my heart that day. He said, "The answer to your prayer is in this very thing . . . that you have loved me with every part of yourself . . . for the part of you that is in your children will some day burst into a flame of love for me. But for the time being, just trust. I am still the Blessed Controller of all things."

6

It happened. I *knew* it would. In a moment of weakness and lousy timing, I told my household about my gentle little cedar waxwings. (I saw three of them on their second visit.) As I suspected, I've been teased, taunted and jeered as to my "blue-winged fletchers" . . . my "flat-chested fledglings," . . . my "flannel-backed bic-flippers" . . . and they now introduce me to their friends as their "fine-feathered fruitcake."

One of my offspring had just mumbled something to the effect that I should use "Big Bird" when autographing my books, when our phone rang. Mark answered, then turned to me while stifling a guffaw, held his hand over the mouthpiece and blurted, "Mother Goose, you're never going to believe this . . . but *Robin's* on the phone!"

And, I did snicker a bit, but anytime Robin calls, it usually means a trauma of some sort, so I went into the bedroom for more privacy. Her strong suicidal tendencies had cropped up again, and she asked me to come over.

"Robin, I'll come . . . but I'm going to ask Gene to come with me. Is Van there? Good, ask him to stick around and we'll be there soon."

Her house was only a short ten minutes away. As we

stepped into her lovely home so bedecked with original charm, so alive with her very own creative touches, I couldn't help wishing *she* looked a little more alive, a little less bird-like, so thin and crumpled in a sobbing heap. We all pulled chairs around her dining room table where she proceeded to nervously chip candle wax from the holders, and attend to her nose . . . depending which happened to be dripping the most profusely at the time. Her husband Van looked so puzzled . . . he couldn't understand her frenzy . . . couldn't understand why a person didn't just see what needed to be done, accept it as a responsibility, then *do it!* Men are terrific that way. Practical. Logical. But alas, sometimes insensitive, too.

Van poured us some coffee. The only thing to break the staccato of her sobs was the tinkling of cups and spoons and a bit of strained, masculine throat-clearing. As always, the men were a bit unnerved by her tears.

Weakly, she began. "I feel so sorry for Van. He'd be so much happier if he were married to someone else."

I responded with a tactful, "Well of course he would! So would my *Gene!* But when Gene committed his life to me at the altar, the vow was 'for better, or for worse' and 'til death do us part,' not 'I'll keep her for as long as she makes me happy!' And remember, these vows were made before God, and not to be taken lightly. Robin, real joy—real fulfillment—comes up out of the core of obedience, out of giving . . . expecting nothing in return."

I guess the emphasis of what I said jarred Gene and Van slightly, as one was wiping coffee off the front of his shirt, and the other one was trying not to smile. Robin vented some more pent-up feelings. The usual stream of "I'm alone too much . . . have full responsibility of the kids . . . he doesn't communicate" came through. And a petulant "we just can't make it together. I know we can't."

Quietly, Gene said, "Yes, you can. If you want to, that is. I've heard Char tell dozens of women that 'I can't' is just a cop-out for 'I don't want to.' But as long as you think 'can't make it,' you're going to psych yourself right into believing it. If you feel 'too much alone' now, think of how 'alone' you will feel when you are divorced. If you think you have too much responsibility of the kids now, who's going to help you out when you live by yourself? And don't think another man is the answer, because most men don't get that excited about raising someone else's children!"

She was now tending candle wax. "Yes," she answered demurely. "I guess that's true . . . but I don't feel loved!" She was now attending to her nose. She continued, "I just don't feel in my heart that I am *loved*," amid more tears.

"Robin, honey," I said, "I hope this doesn't come across as harsh, but nowhere in the Bible does it say we are supposed to *feel* loved! The gentle but firm command is to *give* love, or in other words, to sow love. When we do, God somehow begins to have love surround us, invade and drench us . . . but not when we are seeking after it . . . only when we've given it, unconditionally and with no strings attached.

"And Robin, it's getting late—we need to deal with one more thing here before we leave. Will you please deal squarely with the fact that *it isn't so much your being concerned that Van would be happier with another woman so much as your refusing to verbalize the fact that you feel you would be happier with another man!*"

She sobbed with her head upon her arms. We put our hands on her shaking shoulders and prayed, then left her and Van alone. The wound had been probed, the poison released, now God could begin to heal.

7

To think there was a time in my life, many decades ago, when possibly the heaviest anxiety I had to endure was whether or not my seams were straight. Those were the carefree days of running boards, pompadours, unsplittable atoms, Glenn Miller, and the traditional sprinkling of acne.

Now I am the mother of six, the wife of one, the sister of multitudes, and the grandmother of three. Naively, I thought life would get easier when the children got married. It doesn't get easier. It just gets shorter.

And human nature has such a bent toward always wanting what you can't have. When your children were little, did you ever suffer prickles of guilt because you felt this awful something whisper inside of you "how I wish they were grown"?

I remember a time in particular when I was nearly beside myself (or so I thought) with responsibilities. I went to my doctor in tears. "What's wrong with me?" I complained. "I'm practically a basket case and all these pious little old ladies are patting me on the back and saying, 'Now dearie, these are the best days of your life!' Makes me want to throw my sterilizer at them!"

Tenderly, as he was taking my blood pressure, he smiled

and said, "They've forgotten. That's all."

And, because they've forgotten, they want what they can't have—their little ones back again. I used to go around muttering, "I'd give them two whole days. Two days of chaos, and they'd quit talking about 'the good old days.' " I've always said that the hardest thing I've ever done for my Lord was to raise these six children. And sometimes I wonder if they really got "raised." I think "being propped up and supported while growing" would be more accurate. And may a thousand neighborhood children invade my pantry if I leave you with the impression that I didn't love or enjoy my brood. It's just that there were times that coping seemed impossible—probably because I talked myself into thinking it was all impossible, as it's always easier to believe a lie Satan is trying to lay on you, than to fortify yourself with the Word of God that says, "I can do all things through Christ which strengtheneth me." I actually psyched myself into immobility many times, because of such negative thinking. I have since learned to latch on to the present moment, live it to the hilt, praising God in it, and reaching out to the next moment with eagerness. Moments lived with zest make for joy-filled days. And it is all possible, as long as you don't let those two robbers overtake you—fear of future or regrets of the past. Once they rob you of the joy of the moment, you are in for trouble.

Yes, I loved my children—still do, amazingly. But due to the somewhat indescribable aura that accompanies parenthood, I had this dreadful fear that having raised my six, saluted my Captain, discharged my responsibilities as done, signed, sealed and delivered, I'd probably reject my grandchildren. Politely, of course. I was certain that I'd smile and coo over them as any interested grandparent should.

But now I want to share a tremendous secret with you. . . .

19

Although I am almost totally anatomically ignorant, I have made a scientific discovery that has probably already changed the world, and no one knows it! It has something to do with a little internal appendage in a woman's midsection that no one knows anything about. It is shaped like a tightly closed rose bud, that lies there dormant until—oh, wonder of wonders!—you catch sight of that very first grandchild! Then, the love of God fans it into the sweetest aroma that just seems to pervade every part of your being, filling you with a necessary substance called grandmotherliness. Then, as the days go by, and that child begins to wrap you around his delightful, chubby little finger, you realize at last *why* you had children—and you tell them, gleefully—so that you could have *grandchildren*. And they just grin, and know that you don't really mean a word of it. But nonetheless they humor you because—who knows—now maybe they, too, will have grandchildren someday!

8

The mystery of grandparenting seems to be all wrapped up in the proverb that reads, "Children's children are the crown of old men." (A verse I quote to my dear husband often when I think he needs it. So happy it doesn't say old women.)

The entrance of each grandchild heralds in something so precious . . . and so writable! Our little Kari René was the first to break the sound barrier. Because of her refusal to make her way down into the birth canal, she came by Caesarean section. God, for His own reasons, permitted her to take up life on our planet with a hereditary blood disease that no one on either side of the family ever knew existed! How dreadfully long were those months until the disease was completely diagnosed . . . how paralyzing the fears that crept into our minds. And how glorious was the news that it could be controlled by transfusions and the removal of her spleen when she is five or six. (That gives plenty of time for God to do a miracle so surgery won't be necessary!)

She was the first grandchild on both sides of the family, so her birth announcement had to be special. Here it is:

'Twas the day after Easter when all
through Mom's tummy,

Not a pain was found stirring in my
poor tired Mommy.

The rubber gloves hung by the scalpel
with care—just in case Dr. Middleton
needed them there.

And I, I was nestled in Mommy, in bed,
while visions of doctor bills raced
through Dad's head.

So Mom in her I.V.'s and Doc in green gown,
all settled back to see if I wouldn't
"come down."

When out on the monitor my heart made such a
clatter, The nurses all
rushed out to see what was the matter!

Quick as lightning it happened—Dad's
mind's in a whirl! A Caesarean debt
and a shout, "It's a GIRL!"

Kari René Engle
daughter of Terry and Jan Engle
wishes to thank you all for your prayers and
concern regarding her delayed entrance into this
world . . .

(parents and grandparents all bragging nicely).

Aimee Nicole's (Nikki) arrival was special to me also,
because my daughter-in-law wanted me with her in the labor

22

room along with my son Don and her mother (a fact that warmed my heart considerably). When I queried her to be sure I heard right, I said, "Me? She, who becomes ill when cleaning a chicken?"

She gave me a Madonna-like smile and said, "Yes, you. In fact, I think I'd like a brass band! I don't intend doing this bit very often!"

And oh, how those hours in that labor room drew us all together. With two mothers standing by, Don had leisure for pacing. And pacing. And caring. And perspiring. At one point he came into the room, and they were giving Barb a whiff of oxygen. He looked my way, ran his hands through his hair and blurted out, "What did she do? Try to bite someone?"

But we all came through "Lamazingly" well. (At one point, Don muttered, "Still can't figure out why I have to pay that doctor so much money and do all the work myself," and with that Barb *really* groaned!)

Well, little Thaddeus Allen's coming on the scene was a bit milder, because we knew he would be coming Caesarean because of Kari's setting the precedent. How we felt the presence of the Lord as we prayed with Jan, patted her face, took a peek at the clock and knew that within minutes the Holy Spirit would usher a little darling to us! The Psalmist said, "You took me safely from my mother's womb" (Ps. 22:9 TLB).

We stayed at the hospital until we knew Jan and baby were both doing fine and until we felt we'd expelled the necessary amount of "oo's" and "ah-h-h-h's" in front of the nursery window to help dispel any insecurity Thad might be experiencing. At a given moment, Gene quietly looked at me, and I at him . . . he said, "Guess we'd better go now . . . need to get back to work."

We were walking to the car in the parking lot, when I heard

Gene say, "Hi there, Barry!"

I turned as the so-called Barry walked beyond us, and I turned to Gene, "That isn't the Barry we went to school with, is it?"

"Yes," said Gene.

In my typical shy way, I said, "Barry! So good to see you!"

He walked to me, grinned his crooked grin and said, "Hi, Char! Say, I read both your books. You've really got something there. Even thought about getting in touch with you guys—say, seems a bit ironic, doesn't it? That I should have thought about getting in touch with you, and here you are when I'm about to commit myself into the psych ward?"

With that, he crumpled into a sobbing heap. Quickly, my arm was around him. I called for Gene, then said, "Barry, you don't have to do it right this minute—come home for a cup of coffee at the Potterbaums'."

Limply, he got into our car and we met Lu, the pastor, at our house. What a scene it was! I told Lu later that I felt as though I should have been working on a tent as we all shared, because this must have been much like it happened to Paul, Aquila and sensible little Priscilla. Later, as I shared with Jan, she said, "Oh, mom! Just think! A few minutes earlier or later . . . you'd have missed him."

"Honey, it wasn't our appointment, it was God's. His timing is always right. We only have to be milling about this old hurting world, bearing an expectant love within us, and He will bring the people across our paths who need that love. He is the balm, the director, the coordinator of our circumstances. Our availability to Him will always be put to good use. His threading the miraculous throughout the mundane is what makes life so exciting. See, you had your baby on the delivery-room table, and we had ours over the luncheon table."

For Barry did turn his heart and life over to Christ that day. And I'm happy to tell you that about two months later, his wife came back to him and their marriage was restored.

I just never dreamed that tent-mending or grandparenting could be so delightful!

9

Springtime means more than just influenza, poison ivy, crabgrass and paint peeling to us. For three years now, springtime has ushered in a new grand-baby for us. Naturally, this has meant any number of given trips to various hospitals in the area. On a recent excursion to the maternity ward, Don and I were about to get into an elevator to visit Barb and three-day-old Aimee Nicole. I was looking down the corridor as I absent-mindedly bent over the drinking fountain, somehow missing a remark Don made. When I snapped the lever of what I supposed was a drinking fountain shut, I realized that Don's hissed comment was a painful *"Mother! That's* an *ash*tray!"* as something dusty and distasteful invaded my nostrils and left eyebrow. I giggled, motioned Don—who wasn't giggling—into the elevator and told him I'd be up soon, and made my way to the ladies' room. Besides, I had that nagging feeling that I knew the girl who'd just preceded me into the lounge. I was certain it was an old school friend. Sure enough—we almost collided.

"Min! How good to see you!" And it *was* good. As we talked I confirmed what I'd heard—that she was a very able Bible teacher with a class meeting in her home. A large one, in fact. About forty women . . . and what a joy to know that she was feeding them superbly from the riches of God's Word. We'd been very close friends many years ago, and probably still would be except that she had moved quite some distance away.

And, because of our closeness, I said, "Min, I sent you a copy of my book . . . assumed I must have had the wrong address as I never heard from you." Which, as I look back now, may have been just a ruse. I really think I was trying tactfully to say, "Min, I poured my heart out in a book, and I wanted you to take its pulse."

I was a bit stunned when I heard her reply. "Oh, Char, I got it, but I've never read it. You see, I encourage the women in my Bible study not to read books, as I don't want them to get hung up on personalities."

"Oh, yeah. I see. . ." I lied. We said goodbye, and I made my way thoughtfully to the maternity ward. Inwardly, I was communing. *"Father, I need just a quiet moment to choke and splutter. Lord, where would I be today if I hadn't listened so carefully at the knee of A. W. Tozer? Or rubbed shoulders with the thought life of C.S. Lewis? Martin Luther? Or hadn't brushed the cheek of St. Francis de Sales? Where would I be today, if I hadn't felt your sweet presence via the pens, the minds, of your great ones whose thoughts have been preserved for us? Where would I be, if their yearning for you hadn't ignited my own heart until it could flame brightly with your love?"*

As I made my way down the sterile corridor, I couldn't help thinking how difficult it would be to have a deeper relationship with Christ without personality involvement. Even in the Gospels, the personalities of Matthew, Mark, Luke, John, and Peter, come through! If God had wanted to find us aside from personalities, He could have put a giant tape recorder in the sky running night and day, quoting

Scripture! But the letter of the law kills . . . it is the Spirit that giveth life. Yes, the Spirit of God enclosed in earthen vessels. In essence, the character of Christ can only be manifested through a personality! Hers, mine, Tozer's, Lewis's . . . through the personality of that tender nurse over there caring for that helpless baby. . . .

I arrived just in time to see the babies. We "oohed" and "ahhed" over little Aimee Nicole . . . then Barb looked at me and said, "Is today Ash Wednesday?"

Innocently, I chirped, "No, I don't think so. . . ."

But when I caught the grin on both of their faces, I murmured, "Oh, my. Where's the ladies' room up here?"

10

I don't know which is more depressing . . . hearing a clunky thud that tells you that thirty pounds of soiled teenage laundry is plummeting down the clothes-chute . . . or walking into an elegant dress shop, only to find out they stop—just short of your size! Only mildly depressing, to be sure, and fortunately, I've learned how to deal with depression. As to the laundry, I just quietly thank and praise God for responsibilities, and that the teenagers who tossed it down were healthy, able-bodied, and caring enough to toss it down. As to the dress shop, I just "accept" myself as I am and seek another store with a more expansive line in a less expensive vein.

But I'll have to admit, the pressures of the age we live in are peculiar. The Phillips translation cautions us not to allow the world around us to "squeeze you into its mold" yet, every time I pick up a contemporary how-to book, the author seems to be checking out whether or not I've molded over to their way of thinking yet. In most cases, I haven't.

Never once have I thought of being alarmed if Gene were to catch me with paint smears on my nose, devoid of make-up. (And here is the best definition I've ever heard for cosmetics: "If one feels deficient, then by all means one should. . . make up.") And though we have nothing against frills, lace and candlelight, I'm just as confident of his love if I happen to be shrouded in a granny gown or stuffed into a snowmobile suit. (I wore one once, and looked just like a cookie jar.) And I can honestly tell you that the thought of my pirouetting to the door in pink baby-doll pajamas and perky white boots sends us both into hysterics. Actually, most of my attempts at being alluring border on the hilarious. I'll see young, svelte lasses flitting about, hair blowing freely in the breeze, all accenting their lovely slim throats with saucy little scarfs. Once . . . just once, I did likewise. It drew a sympathetic glance from my husband as he remarked how sorry he was to see that I had a sore throat! And whenever I dab on expensive perfume, I somehow always wind up smelling like wallpaper paste and apple pie.

My success with jewelry is about as great. Some women wear their jewelry so elegantly. I don't know what happens to mine, but all my bracelets tend to look like Mason jar lids, and my necklaces all have a way of making me look like a loosely wrapped package!

And I do so hope you are not chalking all this up to a "poor self-image" for you see, it isn't that at all! I'm so delightfully happy to be "me" . . . so happy in knowing that beauty is not dependent upon baubles and beads, but something that comes from within. I've come to truly love and enjoy the inside "me" and given enough time, and prayer, I shall come to accept the outside "me" as well. But I know from experience that a joyful, strong, conformed-to-the-image-of-Christ spirit is more lasting and captivating than shallow, superficial beauty. And perhaps the greatest discovery of all is knowing that as long as I meet my husband's emotional needs, he will think of me as the most gorgeous creature on earth! He might be hard-pressed to tell you why, or not able to put it into words, but his eyes tell me that it is so, when they meet mine across a crowded room.

I remember reading once about a very heavyset woman who was absolutely adored by her husband. Why? Because she praised him, genuinely, in front of his children! He was made to feel like a king, and was consequently willing to treat her like a queen.

I suppose one of the most beautiful tributes to a woman's true beauty comes from an M.D. in Pasadena, Texas. I found this in a "Dear Abby" column many years ago.

> Dear Abby,
> When I was a boy, I recall we had two apple trees. One was beautiful and perfectly formed, but it bore no fruit. The other bore fruit and showed it by its bent and broken limbs. Dad eventually cut down the beautiful but worthless one.
> My wife bore me five beautiful children. Her breasts now droop and her belly shows not-so-lovely stria-gravida("stretch marks") and plenty of them. But she will not be "cut down." She has borne fruit, and to me hers is the most beautiful body on earth.
> Sincerely,
> an M.D. in
> Pasadena, Texas

This isn't intended as a put-down for those of you who are naturally beautiful and well formed, whether or not you've borne children. It is only meant to be a comfort to those who struggle with inferiorities heaped upon us by style-conscious people who care only for what is seen on the outside. There is still a lot to be said about this inner beauty business. What's more, it is lasting, and never goes out of style.

11

And why shouldn't I enter a writing contest? After all, I was a published author, glib with words, confident of my ability and strikingly adventurous. *I'm poised and secure enough to withstand rejection*, I blandly lied to myself as I whipped out the six-page masterpiece that would bring the publishing world adoringly to my feet. Then, I had only to wait patiently until August the first, "notification of winners" day.

At 4:21 A.M. on that illustrious day, I awoke, acutely aware of a dreadful sinus affront complete with every imaginable symptom. I decided to "greet my tribulation as a friend," curl up with a good book, and enjoy the bed rest. Besides, what an ideal excuse to lie close to the phone, awaiting the winner's telegram.

6:48 A.M.—Working and functioning segment of family departed, leaving me free to shape menthol-scented dreams of how I would spend contest award, as I gazed into my vaporizer mist.

7:02 A.M.—Besides envisioning the impact I would have on the entire publishing world, I was also mentally preparing what I would say when the coveted call came. I would let it ring twice, so as not to look too "green." Then, in my most honey-and-lemon-coated voice, I would offer a demure

"Hedoow? Yeds, I'b Bissis Potterbahb . . . I'b what? A widder? How barvedous!" I rehearsed it in several different nasal tones.

8:31 A.M.—Faced dumb facts squarely, that (1) whatever gave me the idea that a telegram should come over the phone? I'd never *gotten* one! (2) My phone was unlisted! (3) Never once had I even hinted my phone number on the submitted manuscript!

8:31½ A.M.—Made my way through the mist slightly encumbered by a bulky vaporizer, tissues, lozenges, inhalators, histamines, vitamins, security blanket, sinus drainage and considerable rasping and choking, to the first floor where I felt I could languish more effectively closer to the doorbell.

10:43 A.M.—Remembered foggily, while tissue-tossing, that I'd read somewhere that "if you could write humor, publishers would beat a path to your door." I felt path should at least be neat and tidy. Swept walk, removed dog bones, skateboard, Coke cans, Beef jerky wrappers, can of worms—dead ones, one dented bike fender, two neighbor children—live ones, and a soggy sock, to the accompaniment of much snorting, sneezing and various indelicate snufflings. But actually, it was all just a ruse, as my main objective was to check out doorbell device.

It was working.

11:53 A.M.—Sluggishly prepared instant potatoes, instant hot dogs and instant pudding for children, and Constant Comment for myself. (Gene said it suited me—to a tea.) All the while constantly commenting to Jamie that he really shouldn't be dragging the dorsal fin that he'd made through the river, as neighbor children were having nightmares and wetting the bed.

2:13 P.M.—Called Western Union to see if they were on

strike.

They weren't.

4:58 P.M.—Remembered that Mickey Rooney always delivered his telegrams on a bike, so resorted to low moaning to keep compassionate children quiet, thus enabling me to better listen for the whirr of a Schwinn, while peeking through the sheers at my window.

5:02 P.M.—Wondered if anyone ever overdosed on vitamin C.

5:04 P.M.—Checked calendar, to make sure I was using current year.

I was.

6:02 P.M.—Sympathetic but starving husband came home, touched my forehead and murmured, "We deserve a break today" so *they* all headed for McDonald's.

8:41 P.M.—Called neighbor. "Barge? I'b sedding Bark over with typewriter—puddit id your garage sale toborrow."

10:31 P.M.—Decided that writing books was easier than writing short stories, anyhow.

11:00 P.M.—Took two aspirin and went to bed, wondering if I'd been so foolhardy and confident as to neglect putting a self-addressed envelope in with the manuscript.

1:35 A.M.—Awoke with a start—and a splutter and a gag—reached for pen and pad, and feverishly outlined story about "The Ague and I" for *Health* magazine.

12

So many young mothers have said, "This business of yielding to Christ—I don't understand what it means." And, since Jesus did such an effective job when relating about His "sower that went out to sow" and His "the ground of a certain man brought forth plentifully" I thought I could best explain by putting my answer into story form.

So you see, once upon a nervous breakdown, a certain daughter of the King went fumblingly on her way. She had a tendency to fuss and fume over every circumstance she found herself in. She could be peevish about even unchangeable things like, for instance, the weather! And she was seldom satisfied. Even when she was thin, she thought she was fat. And though her house was adequate, still she complained. She had a fine husband—hardworking, thoughtful, ambitious. But she complained about this, too.

Now, if the truth were but known, our heroine had everything going for her. Why? Because she knew God. But she couldn't be satisfied here either, for she consistently whined around the castle that she didn't feel loved. Well, even though her knowledge of God was very vague, still our heroine had developed a pretty good habit of getting on her knees and talking with God. Granted, her prayers were rather

35

fuzzy and cockleburred, with many "oh, give me's" and heavily scented with a lot of woeful "if only's." You see, she'd come to believe that happiness depended upon outward circumstances. If she could just manipulate God and others around her to conform to her way of thinking, and if she could just get others to do as she wanted them to, why of course she could be happy! Little did she know that this attitude stemmed straight from the dreadful pit of hell—that this desire to control her circumstances, and yes, even the hearts and minds of others, came from the awful, awesome proclamation by Lucifer that he would be "like God." For if she controlled others, if they did exactly as she thought they should—would she then not be in complete control, setting herself up as a god?

Well, fortunately for our little princess, her Father the almighty King overlooked this proneness to control, and looked even deeper into her heart. He knew that the deep yearnings of her heart had been planted there by His Spirit, and all these other "waste products" would be burned up by the fire of the Holy Spirit, once He was given control. So the King wasn't nearly as concerned as were the other subjects of this kingdom she was trying to set up for herself. For sadly, you see, she made the lives of others quite miserable. She made her husband, the handsome prince, feel most inadequate. She was constantly making demands of him that he couldn't fulfill. Her children were not happy, either, you see, because the princess had been given the important responsibility of establishing a happy atmosphere in the castle, and she was not fulfilling her sacred duties in this area!

But one day, our fretful little princess was crying. She saw that her garden was completely overrun with nettles, briars and weeds. The fruit of the Spirit she'd so hoped she could harvest and bring before the King were being choked and strangled. With great determination (referred to in the kingdom as "an act of the will") she set about untangling the vines that had grown around the fruit trees. And as she worked, she suddenly stumbled upon something—oh, see! She found the keys of the kingdom! She was ecstatic as she fondled them! There they were in all their shimmering glory, just waiting to unlock the rusted chambers of her heart! The biggest and the heaviest key of them all was marked "acceptance." With great care and perseverance, she applied that key to her heart, but found it needed coaxing and persistence. But gloriously, it seemed to be the master key—the one that would make the others "fit." As she hesitantly began to accept herself, with all her limitations and weaknesses, her abilities and uniqueness, she found it quite easy to accept her husband, just as he was—and wonder of wonders, she found that the very essence of yielding to Christ meant "accepting" circumstances *as they were* and as having come directly from God's hand, fashioned in love for the very shaping and molding of her life. Now, when she got up from her knees, she understood that if she really meant it when she prayed, "Lord, I give you my life, my heart," the way to prove it was to get up from her knees and accept all the circumstances as being meted out by a just and loving God.

One of the other keys was tagged "giving." She found out that "giving, expecting nothing in return" entitled her to a deeper abundance of love than she could ever have hoped for, or imagined. She found out that nowhere had she ever been commanded to "feel" loved, but only commanded to *give* love. Well, needless to say, the discovery of these keys had a profound effect upon the princess's little family. They all clapped their hands in glee, as love and joy began to fill up the castle. And, as the writer of this little story and the clap-happy princess are one and the same, I can honestly tell you that they all lived haphazardly together, right up until at least the penning of this story, continually "keyed-up" and ready for anything the King commanded!

13

I have a friend who is visually impaired, enough so that she is considered blind. She paid me the honor of asking me to accompany her to a banquet for the blind. I arrived at her home, helped her with some finishing touches, assured her that her shoes matched, checked her all over, only to discover she'd sat in something sticky, so I began to enthusiastically swipe away at the spot with cold water. The spot disappeared, but then it looked as though she'd wet her pants. I giggled, "Louise, do you have a blow dryer?"

She groaned, "Only the kind you set on a table and stick your head under."

I sputtered, "That will have to do, but it's not your head we're going to stick anyplace," as I hysterically wedged her derriere into the large dome of the hair dryer we'd set on a kitchen chair. We recovered from the hysteria, trying to muster up a measure of dignity so as to appear at least a bit elegant in our long dresses . . . even if she was sweltering in the coat we'd decided she should wear to cover up the wet spot for the time being.

At the banquet, we were asked to face the flag and sing "God Bless America." Now realize, half of these people were blind. (The other half were the sighted ones who'd taken them.) I stood up, and properly faced the podium, assuming that that would naturally be a reasonable place to keep a flag. I was amazed to see all the people literally singing directly to me—smiling and oh, so friendly. Until I froze and numbly realized that, good heavens, the flag was directly behind me!

She wondered what they'd be serving, and I concluded that if what my mother told me was true, it would be carrots . . . and it was. The meal was terrific and the fellowship superb. Our evening was topped off with another burst of insanity as all the laughter necessitated a trip to the ladies' room, where she managed somehow to lose part of her hearing aid in the toilet booth. Of course, she couldn't hear me at all as I was trying to say, "What's wrong?" at the top of my lungs. I made my way into her booth, and you can imagine my relief when I found the missing part caught in the fold of her dress . . . and not where I feared. (After all, I didn't want her to get swimmer's ear!) She and I both decided that it was a very good thing that neither of us drank, as we got into so-o-o much trouble *sober*. And if a merry heart doeth good like a medicine, we came very close to "overdosing" on that memorable night.

14

What does one do about the tingling at the
Nape of the neck
When the doorbell rings
And the hot chocolate cups are still cemented to the
     counter top
And a day-old sock is still draped on a kitchen stool rung
And you glance at the clock and see, good heavens! it's
     11:15 A.M.
And you really should be dressed, but aren't,
And to ignore the bell would be deceiving,
And to make excuses would be weak?

You swallow convulsively, quiet all the "shoulds" running
     rampant in your mind,
And sigh with relief as you see it's
Your sister, who really, of all people, should understand.

We sit and chat, and gleefully,
I start to see my house through her twinkling eyes as she
     remarks how perfectly the red legs of the ironing board
Match the candles on the dining room table.
And I look prim and say, "It's a Bicentennial exhibition,

41

you see . . .
   Otherwise, I'd take it down."

And she will say "I see you've finally trained the kids to use
   the door in back. . . ."

Puzzled, I retorted, "How can you tell?"
Chokingly, she parries with "the candlesticks. They are all
   leaning toward the *front* door!"

Yes, the ironing board stands at attention for the duration
   of Laurie's teenage years
And the lampshades are dreadfully at ease for the duration
   of child-rearing years
And the candles *do* lean Westward, Ho.

But to us, it is home.
Secure, lived-in, roomy
And with all the furniture really "in" because of its natural
   look.

Yes, it's home, and to leave it gives me
Spasms of homesickness before I even pull out of the
   driveway.

What does one do about the tingling at the
Nape of the neck when the doorbell rings?
Blame it on menopause,
I guess.

15

"More than likely," I mused, "they will have to pry my fingers loose" as I envisioned myself standing in front of my first (of three) meeting in Cleveland, with the steering wheel still in my hands. I'd been reduced to driving, as the airports throughout the Midwest were closed due to a blizzard. It would have been a natural thing just to cancel out the meetings, but somehow, I didn't have peace in my spirit about that, either. However, I hadn't reckoned on . . . *car trouble!*

I felt some womanly anxiety building up as I steadily lost acceleration on the toll road. I'd been sailing along at fifty-five, but gradually lost down to forty-five—forty—then found myself lopping along at a pitiful thirty miles an hour! I turned on my emergency lights as doubts assailed me. I stared out into the pitch blackness of the night, seeing only an occasional swirl of snow . . . and very little traffic as the temperature was sub-zero.

"Father?" I prayed. *"Did I miss your voice somewhere? Was it my senseless will that goaded me on? Well, no matter . . . I am here at this point in time because of a decision I made, whether it lined up with your will or not, and you've promised never to leave me nor forsake me . . . so I'll try to*

get rid of this forsaken feeling as you get me, hopefully, at least to the next exit. And if you'd also provide a repair station and a motel, I'd be most grateful!

The thoughts of standing forlornly beside a broken-down car on a deserted toll road didn't come anywhere near to my idea of how to spend a quiet winter evening!

Well, a band of ministering angels *did* push me to the next exit, and there, big as life, was the necessary station . . . closed for the night. But also, as requested, the shelter I longed for in a motel right across the street, where I could "come apart" (lest I *come* apart).

Needless to say, I sniveled a little bit there before the Lord, but the cry of my heart was, "Father, I need so much to know that you are *in* all of this!" Well, in those next two days, He proved His lovingkindness to me in ways I never could have discovered, had I "copped-out" on those meetings by remaining at home.

First of all, He'd gotten me to an exit that was just one short of my destination. It wasn't too troublesome for contacts in Cleveland to pick me up and taxi me about to various meetings. And as we drove through, in, and around the "arctic regions" of Cleveland, how my heart rejoiced that *I* hadn't been required to drive in that impossible mess!

Secondly, God was stirring up the hearts of twenty mental health patients (suffering from depression who were a part of a government plan called "Recovery") to come to the main luncheon, to hear how I'd learned to cope with depression.

And thirdly, and most importantly, He did manifest himself to me in a very special way . . . by moving upon the hearts of the congregation of one church to "take up an offering." (This was to have been just a "courtesy" call . . . no offering was anticipated.) But from such a small congregation I was overwhelmed to find that they'd given me $58.20! And so, from that offering, I gave them back $2.00 for a collect phone call, leaving me with a balance of $56.20. Can you even begin to imagine my joy and excitement when I picked up my car and discovered that the repair charge was $56.29! (Especially when I recalled that the actual phone charge had been $1.90! That accounted for the missing 9¢!) My heart was so warmed by this "show of love." I didn't even notice the sub-zero weather . . . I was only aware of the purr of my smooth-running car, of my contented heart, and His loving, eternal presence!

16

Jennifer isn't quite five, but she proved to me that she has great wisdom. She lives in Key Biscayne, Florida, and I had the pleasure of spending some time with Jennifer recently as I had speaking engagements in that area. (Her mother and father are "Beth and Bert" of my first book, *If You See Lennie*.)

I'm an early riser, so I'd been up some time and from my bedroom, I could hear that Jennifer had a nasty, croupy cough. A cough so familiar to my ears in Indiana, but I'd hardly expected to hear something like that against a background of palm fronds and falling coconuts.

When Jennie got out of bed, I put my hand under her chin. Her eyes looked a bit glassy, like children do when they are feverish. I said, "Honey, you've such an awful cough . . . does mother have any cough syrup I can give you? I'm afraid you're really coming down with something. . . ." She looked very knowledgeable and croaked, "No, but I'll show you what we use." She took my hand and led me into the front room. There on a low shelf loaded with artistic antiques was a small vial of oil. She looked up at me with such innocence and trust, brushed her lovely blonde hair away from her face, and gave me these instructions.

"What you do, Auntie Charlene . . . you just take and put some of this oil on your finger and put it up here on my head, and then you pray." And her two chubby hands clasped together cherubically as her little lids fluttered shut and she raised her pixie face toward heaven.

Choking back the usual outburst of laughter, I joyously prayed, "O Father—forgive me—and thank you so much for her simple faith. Heal her, Lord, in Jesus' name."

Beth and the children accompanied me to my speaking engagements, then we spent a few days with Beth's mother, Hazel. Other than telling Beth the incident of my little prayer session with Jennie, I forgot about it. Jennie's grandmother Hazel and I shared a room and acted much like giddy teenagers, often talking into the wee hours of the morning. The last night we were together, in the middle of a sentence I sat bolt upright in bed when I heard Jennie clear her throat from the opposite bedroom. Hazel said, "What's wrong?"

I reverently said, "Jennifer—I just remembered. Hazel, we've been together how many—let's see—five days now, and she hasn't coughed *once!* Hazel, that child was really sick when we prayed together. Oh, God is *so* good! I must remember to learn from Jennifer's faith. *I* was going to poke her full of cough syrup. Thank you, Lord . . . you told us 'and a little child shall lead them.' "

17

Being an author is just plain fun. In fact, downright egotistical. And if I didn't know for certain that things were as they should be in my prayer closet, I might be a bit concerned. Plus, my heavenly Father has always surrounded me with the greatest bunch of people in the world, who are solely dedicated to keeping me humble. And He allows so many things to happen to keep me in touch with my humanity. Take yesterday, for instance. I was eating in a posh restaurant with some posh people. I'd very daintily chosen a small chef's salad . . . to impress them, I suppose, as my *real* inclinations leaned a bit more toward lasagna or spaghetti.

Well, when the salad was served, I discovered that the only thing small about it was the round-bottomed bowl it was served in. As to what would happen when I put a blob of gooey dressing on it remained to be seen. But not for long, for in about three seconds the salad "remained to be seen" draped all over the front of me. A piece of cheese on a rim of my Geoffrey Beane glasses, chunks of Roquefort entwined in my jewelry, and the recalcitrant tomato I'd been trying to sever stared at me soggily from my left elbow. I was greatly relieved to know that a particular clown who was always telling me that "after all, it *was* hard to hit a moving target" every time I spilled something down the front of me was not anywhere on the premises. (You'll find me wearing ruffles much of the time, as these can be daintily rearranged when gravy-splotched.)

Times like these bring balance into my life. They offset the flattering moments, like when the stewardesses fluttered all over me on flight #595 between Cleveland and Miami. They'd found out I was an author, had me autograph the copies I gave them in full view of all the other air passengers, and gave me a "Friendly Skybird" hat signed with the names of the entire crew. Believe me, it was quite a heady experience.

But God, being the great equalizer He is, attached a bit of humble pie-in-the-sky to my history when I returned home. I'd pulled up to a gas station and handed the attendant my credit card. He took a look at the name, grinned, and said, "Say, I read your book just the other day." I fluffed my hair a bit and said, "Oh, really? That really makes my day!"

"Yeah," he grunted as he leaned across the windshield and swiped away. "Y' see—my dad's a trash collector, and one day I was helpin' him collect the trash, an' sure enough there it . . ." and in unison we chanted together "was-as-big-as-life!" I was hysterical by the time I drove away, and he was left muttering some apologies and an "Uh, now don't feel bad, I mean my mother read it, and let's see—oh, yeah, my sis—it was a *real* good book, lady."

And I'm envisioning this smelly little mass of papers threaded throughout with dried spaghetti—and maybe some maggots for book worms? Oh, well, the Lord can just recycle my books any old way He wants to. At least it was still bearing some fruit—like peach pits and banana peelings!

18

The dying man before me had been violent and incoherent the day before. But as he seemed to be a bit more rational, his wife had asked me if I wanted to come in and say good-night to him.

Actually, I wanted to say much more than that to him. I wanted to take his face between my hands and say, "Keith, don't you realize you are dying? Do you know what it's doing to your wife and kids as they wonder about your eternal destiny?" But I'd been told he'd have nothing to do with any such talk, so I stood there mutely, wondering what you do when you can't talk about what is most important in everyone's life. I'd also been told that he was very sensitive to touch, so I was surprised when he reached for my hand as he whispered, "Hi, Char." This move so unnerved me, I decided I would throw caution to the wind and "do my thing."

"Keith?" I whispered as I brushed the wet hair from his sweaty brow. "Keith, please let me pray with you before I leave. . . ."

Weakly, he said, "No . . . not just yet." But as I stood there, I saw the tear that crept down his stubbled beard.

I looked at his wife, "Marcia, would you leave us alone,

please?" Her eyes were full of questions, but I knew that she trusted me.

When we were alone, I continued stroking his forehead. He didn't seem to object to this. "Keith? Can you hear me?" *Oh, Keith, please hear me. I know you are an agnostic, but you are dying, and we've so little time left . . .* "Keith, do you know that God loves you?"

"Yes, I know that."

"Keith, He loves you so much more than you can ever know. Could we pray together now?"

Faintly, he answered, "Please. . . ."

I took his hand in mine, hoping he wouldn't notice the tears streaming down my own face, as I prayed, "Father, how helpless I feel. But my faith is in you, Lord, and I know that you can do a work deep down in Keith's spirit. But because of our own weakness, will you somehow, Lord, let us know that everything is all right between you and Keith? Thank you, Father . . . I ask it in Jesus' name."

Quietly, he took my hand and said, "But how can I know that has happened?"

"Do you mean, Keith," I tremulously said, "how can you know that it's all okay between you and the Lord?"

"Yes," he said, his voice barely audible.

I experienced a shiver of joy as I asked, "Keith, would you be willing to repeat a prayer after me? Say the words after me?"

Again, a weak "Yes." And as I led him through the sinner's prayer, I wondered if he wasn't so near death's door that he might even hear the angels rejoicing over the one lost sinner who was found.

All of this took place just ten days ago. Last night, Keith died. He was the husband of my niece, Marcia. She told me that his anger and violence never returned. Keith was born the same year as I was. It truly makes a person ponder . . . and remember how valuable each treasured day is.

19

I woke up to the sound of rain. "Lord, the travel agency was going to be very specific about that . . . they were going to request excellent weather for Virgean to be wheeled from one terminal to the other. The day isn't really going according to our plans. H-m-m."

After a brisk shower to help the adrenalin flow, I got my second shocker for the day, via the telephone. "Char, this is Herb. My mother is sick and won't be able to come and help you clean."

Lord, I hope I learn whatever lesson you are trying to teach me early in this day, as I'm not sure I can handle much more, I thought, as I viewed the messy kitchen, the half-done laundry and the room that needed to be rearranged. "Sure, Herb. Tell her I'll be praying." *Oh, well. I've several hours before Virgean arrives.* Being a drawer-crammer and closet-jammer from way back, I wasn't doing too badly, when I got another phone call. It was still four hours until Virgean's flight was due in, so I thought I was really coming along in good shape.

I received a call from my pastor. "Char? This is Lu—are you ready for this? I just got a call from the airlines, and Virgean's flight was changed—she'll be in in about twenty minutes. . . ."

I was sorry that no one was around to admire the dramatic fall into the nearest chair. "The what said *when?*" I squeaked.

"Twenty minutes," Lu said. "I'll pick her up, if that will help any."

"Yeah . . . yeah, thanks Lu. And take her on a tour of the city . . . show her the church, the water tower, the . . . the parks, the drainage plant . . . pul-lease keep her occupied for a while. And Lu, I don't know what will be meeting you when she gets off the plane . . . I mean, she told me she'd be wearing a backpack, and you know, her motorcycle accident and all—she might be wearing a black leather jacket and an Indian headband, for all I know. See ya' Lu."

Thus began the first day of Virgean's entrance into our lives.

Virgean had been an aspiring young actress. She'd toured the states and Europe, and was about to settle down to a vibrant teaching career in creative dramatics when she decided to try out a Moto-cross track. She'd always been so high-spirited and adventurous. She loved the feel of the wind and the power of the cycle beneath her knees . . . just one turn around the track, that was all. One simple pulsating turn . . . one free-wheeling, life-tingling turn, and she would be satisfied . . . never mind that they were telling her to slow down. She was feeling her independence. She was a free spirit, wasn't she? She'd handled herself in dangerous situations before, hadn't she? Oh, Virgean . . . sweet innocence, darling girl. If you'd known that your life would be altered, would you . . . ? But it's all over now.

And as Virgean looks in retrospect now, at that broken heap of humanity lying there, so still, motionless, she says, "That was the death of the then-known Virgean Friedrichs."

For three long suspenseful months, Virgean lay in a

hospital flailing about in total unconsciousness. Her mother remarked that Virgean entered even into her unconsciousness wholeheartedly, as she did everything else. Grave months. Hopeless months. Doctors shook their heads, and dropped their eyes when her parents came near. How could they tell them that she would probably always be the vegetable they saw every day?

And when she awoke, she found herself imprisoned in a body that had once thrilled multitudes, but now wouldn't obey even her simplest wishes. She couldn't put a spoon to her mouth. She couldn't gulp. It was like living a nightmare daily, when she heard the horrible monotone that kept escaping from her lips when she tried to communicate. She, whose acting had been said to have had the "sensual quality" of an Ingrid Bergman was now reduced to a wailing creature as dependent upon others as a newborn babe. She, who had so treasured her independence.

Gone, seemingly forever, were the two things she gloried in the most . . . her speech and her graceful movement. But when she became conscious again, something else had entered her very being. It is difficult for Virgean to put it into words, but somehow . . . by some spiritual osmosis, as her mother faithfully read the Word daily to her, not even knowing if Virgean could hear her during her unconsciousness, Virgean gave herself to Christ.

And even today, when Virgean visits nursing homes, she pleads with people to be very careful about what they say in front of those who are comatose, or even semiconscious.

Well, for the time being, God has moved Virgean into our household. She and I are learning valuable lessons by sharing life together. When God sent Virgean to us in that precious disabled body, He also lovingly included something else in with the package. Two loving, willing,

55

eager-to-be-used hands. Hands that move slowly always, and often haltingly . . . but hands that were imbued with the gift of helps . . . hands that mend, make banners, stack blocks for children, bake cookies, clean counter tops, load dishwashers, sew beautiful garments, fold clothes, and, oh yes . . . sometimes those uncoordinated hands spill water, knock things over. But so do my somewhat coordinated ones. But I feel that her hands are special . . . her body is special. For it bears the marks of the ownership of the Lord Jesus Christ, and she belongs to Him. Her hands are His hands, as she works . . . weeps . . . and folds them in prayer to Him. I praise God for those hands . . . and for Virgean.

20

During an especially busy time recently, my sister Lauraine warned, "Char, you need to be careful—I think you're spreading yourself too thin. . . ."

I cast my eyes downward, hoping she'd mistake it for humility, but actually, I was getting a bird's-eye view of both hips! I grinned. "Lauraine, it would be impossible for me to *ever* spread myself *thin*. You can color me matronly, dub me as 'healthy,' well-rounded, full-bodied . . . but you'll never be able to spread me thin!" We giggled good-naturedly together, finished our coffee and said good-bye. As I walked her to the door, I did my usual thing. As I approached the full-length mirror in the entryway, I inhaled until my face was contorted; mumbled a breathless "S' long" and secretly wondered if I was building up powerful lungs or would I just die someday of apoplexy due to an underdose of oxygen.

I've even joined the masses of Americans that are jogging. Only my gait is somewhere between jogging and walking so I call it "jo-king," because the whole time I'm pushing ever forward, pounding that merciless pavement until my fillings work loose, I'm muttering, "They've *got* to be kidding! Whoever said this was *fun!*" (Just the other day, a fun-loving nephew nearly croaked when he heard what I was up to. He bellowed, "*You?* Running? Whadya do? Wear a hard hat with a blinking yellow light and carry a wide-load sign?" For that, I served him a cup of olive green coffee.)

But I know for a fact, that if I'd maintained all the weight loss I've experienced down through the years, by my calculations, I should be able to fly in formation with Tinker Bell. But slow metabolism, long hours at the typewriter, plus uncommitted taste buds keep the scales in a constant state of indecision.

My son Don gets downright indignant when he hears me talk about dieting. "Ma, what ails you? Mothers aren't supposed to run around looking like sixteen-year-olds! Especially grandmothers!" But I guess I never accept all this at a deep gut level. I find myself eating everything that says "thin." Wheat *thins,* leci*thin, thin* spaghetti, just any*thin'* I can get my hands on.

The other day, I met my friend Lynn. I hadn't seen her for some time, and she looked so great! The last time I'd seen her, she looked nearly emaciated. Granted, she was into a smaller dress size that graced a tiny waistline, but her eyes looked like cellar windows in a brownstone.

"Hey, Lynn," I spluttered. . . . "Welcome back to junk food and the land of the living. The last time I saw you, I didn't know whether to give you my last bite—or last rites."

She made a pixie face and said, "Talk about frustration! I feel better when I'm heavier, but I look better when I'm thinner. But my husband said, 'Lynn, you were a little plump when I married you. I liked you that way. When you concentrate so much on your figure, you become a different person. I resent all those nights at the "Y" . . . you just aren't the same Lynn to me. . . .' When he said all this, I had to ask myself, 'If I'm not losing weight for him, then who *am* I losing weight for?' And suddenly I realized that the world was trying to squeeze me into its mold—that I must have been worrying about what other women thought about me—I was playing their game of *competition!* Once I found out the name of the game, I was ready to call it quits!"

"Well," I commented, "like I keep telling Gene—a pleasant face will do much more for the kingdom of God than a shapely figure."

She giggled. I know she thought of that as a cop-out. "No, I'm serious . . . well, almost. But it *is* in our face that we show forth the glory of God—or the lack of it." The more I said, the more she roared.

But recently, Gene said, "Char, your being thin wouldn't cause any of us to love you any more than we do now, would it?" A sweet balm to that part of me that's striving to accept this given exterior.

We have another friend whose wife has an obvious weight problem, and out of curiosity I asked him (not in her presence) if it was a problem for him. He looked thoughtful for a moment, and said, "I can't see it as important, one way or the other. When you fall in love with a person, you fall in love with the *whole* person, not just one aspect of their being, say, the looks, for instance, of a person." I felt it all to be very heartwarming and reassuring.

I guess the two things that we women need to keep uppermost in our minds is that: 1) Our men do not see us as we see ourselves. They look for a warm inner spirit—one that expresses gratefulness and quiet contentedness, where we are so prone to see ourselves in terms of physical attractiveness and stylishness. And: 2) The most important thing is not to think so much in terms of how we look, but rather in terms of making the people around us feel comfortable. Are they relaxed when they are with us? Do they seek our company? And what do they really want? They want to see Jesus—in us.

Everyone is having a struggle of one kind or another. We all need recognition, approval, love, acceptance, encouragement, and we all need friends. Once I'd made the discovery that all human beings were crying out to have their needs met, I decided that God hadn't put me on earth to be a showpiece anyhow, but an instrument of His peace, a means of helping to meet those needs.

The doorbell just rang—it was the paper boy. On my way to the door, I stuck out my tongue at the full-length mirror.

21

Communication. So glibly discussed, but so little practiced. Naively, I stated in my first book that communication was "two hearts willing to beat in harmony." And later, I knew it needed a deeper definition. Something a bit meatier, like "speaking the truth in love." But Gene and I garbled all that up by thinking it meant to truthfully shred the soul of the other by mentioning all the actions of the other that irked us. Then, as we nestled a bit more snugly into maturity, we finally discovered that real communication is discovering and relating our own feelings to one another . . . attacking the problem, not the person.

Sounds simple, doesn't it? Great in theory, but hard to put into practice. Hard, because the process of unlearning the dreadful game we'd been forced to play, that awful game of covering up our true feelings out of fear of hurting the other person. But whenever we employ fear, whose territory have we entered into? Perfect love casts out fear, so the truth spoken in love need never be accompanied by fear. Pain, perhaps, as establishing relationships can often be painful, but when fear prevents us from sharing at a deep gut level then honesty and transparency and intimacy go right out the window.

The other day, I was sharing with my pastor some problems I'd had in counseling others. You see, my pastor is not only my shepherd, but my mentor, my crying towel, my sounding-board and my encourager.

"Lu, my greatest difficulty is in teaching women how to communicate with their mates. Somehow, those mates fail to hear the messages the women are sending them. Why do we women have such a time getting our men to understand what we are trying to say?"

He pushed a bit away from his desk and sighed, "Char, it's probably one of the saddest results of the Fall. I think God had originally intended that men would fully realize what their sensitive, tender mates were trying to say, but when we were separated from God we were also separated from one another. Only in God, and out of His goodness, is it possible for us even to glean a little understanding of how you delicate women think. We suffer from an awkwardness when it comes to expressing our feelings. I can tell another man how to relate to his wife, and yet because of my own busy-ness I often fail to relate to my own wife, Barb, the way I should.

"For instance, the other day she'd left to teach school. A few minutes later she pulled back into the driveway. My heart leaped for joy when I saw her coming back into the house. But did I bother to tell her that? No . . . just mumbled 'forget something?' and never took the time to tell her how delighted I was to see her again, if only for a few moments. And this morning, she was so full of things she wanted to share—deep things, about her longing for more of God. But did I take the time to tell her how deeply moved and blessed I was? No. I just disinterestedly said, 'Well, yeah . . . okay. Maybe we can take an hour or so tonight after the kids are in bed.' And Char, do you know what it means to me to have Barb sitting in on my teaching sessions? It means everything to me! But I don't tell her. And I could *kick* myself for not taking the time to say the things I know she longs to hear. And I know that most men feel this way . . . they just aren't free enough in Christ to verbalize what they feel . . . perhaps we are afraid you women won't know how to handle it."

I interrupted him. I took his hand in mine. "Lu, do me a favor. Do *all* of womanhood a favor. Go home and tell Barbara the things you just told me . . . so that somewhere, somehow, one woman will hear those things that her heart craves so much to hear. And allow me to write it up as a memorial to all women everywhere . . . that one man dared to tell his wife what all women long to hear."

Lu said, "Char, I will. I promise." And then we prayed . . . for families everywhere . . . that in the Spirit they would be freed to communicate the truth in love, free to remind each other that after all, they *were* on the same side, serving the same captain. Free to remind one another that the battle was always raging but the scene, the battlefront, shifts from time to time. But our battle is not with people, but with evil spirits that harass, disrupt, plant suspicion, and keep from the truth . . . the truth that must be, can be, has to be, spoken in love.

22

It was one of those times when the weight of my sinfulness was crushing me. I was sloshing around in Romans 7, tripping over sins and bumping my shins on the law, momentarily forgetting that I could move into Romans 8, any time I wanted to, stripping myself of the condemnation I was wallowing in. Everything melted into one ugly lump and my pride was too great to tell anyone in the body of Christ that I had a need. After all, I was a vibrant, mighty, effective counselor of women—how dared I have a problem?

I knew the pastor would be dropping by to talk with Virgean. Everything inside of me was screaming for some counsel, some word of encouragement, but the enemy clobbered that with "Who do you think you are? She needs to talk and you don't! And besides, you'd have to admit that I've got you cornered, and that wouldn't make your God look very good, now would it?"

In just a few short minutes, the familiar knock at the door. I put on the front that I felt was necessary, mumbled a hurried "hello" and disappeared to the kitchen, but took the time to pop my head back into the living room to say, "Let me know when you pray—I'd like to be in on that," and walked away, only to hear the two of them say, "Well, then come on back in—we're going to pray now." With great decorum and self-control, I seated myself on a footstool by the two of them. With that same sweet spirit of meekness that clothed Jesus, Lu began quietly to pray. Little did he know it, or even knows to this day how he used the gift of wisdom that God wanted me to hear. And softly, ever so softly, I experienced great gulps of His love as His freeing body ministry began, and I began to share my hurts, fears and failures.

"Char," Lu said, "I just want to remind you that Jesus went this way, too. And He went even lower—so much lower that none of us will ever know the depths He went to, there in the garden. But Char, He passed you on the way down. Time means nothing to Him, and when He passed you on His way down, He waved and said, 'You can make it, because I'm going even lower so that I can bring you back up!' Char, He knows all about your evil thoughts. We all have them. He knows of your lack of love and He also knows you've heaped a lot of condemnation on yourself, but He'll walk with you in that too. And there, entrenched so firmly in the midst of you is the forgiving Christ, the redeeming Christ, the resurrected Christ. And He wants you to know that you don't have to feel the weight of your sinfulness like this. He's paid for it all! None of it will ever be put to your account. Char, I'm not going to give you any spiritual talk about how you 'should' be walking in victory—how you 'should' be always 'on top' of the circumstances. I'm just telling you that Jesus walks with you in it, and through it all—and Virgean and I will, too." And how sweetly were the three of us assembled there, basking in His light and love, fellowshiping with one another, and how effectively did His blood cleanse me from all my sin. The warmth of His presence and His Word told us that a book of remembrance was being written before Him as we shared, fearing the Lord and thinking upon His name.

23

Wow. I'm awed and dumbstruck. I just talked with the publisher and made the exhilarating discovery that you, the busy, harried breathless darlings I write for, have actually given me some kind of 'vote of confidence' by gobbling up what I write! (It is a great wonder to my children that anyone would read anything I've ever written, much less *pay* to hear what I might have to say at a luncheon!)

But lest you think it is all laurels and hurrahs, I'm going to tell you about the odyssey of an oddity. (The oddity was the most recent manuscript, *Thanks Lord, I Needed That!*) You see, a publishing company in England wanted my book. Their reasoning sounded so good .... They had a joint publishing agreement with a reputable firm in this country . . . and my little gluttonous nature responded with "Why not? Kill two countries with one manuscript? Good business." And so Gene and I prayed, and both felt it to be a sound venture.

It was a bitterly cold day when Gene offered to mail the manuscript off on his way to work. He put it in the Pinto, opened the garage door, and turned the car on so it could warm up while he made a phone call. When he went back to the garage, he let out a war-whoop that brought me flying out of the kitchen as we almost collided on his way to the phone. "Get your clothes on! Car's on fire" as he nervously dialed the fire department. Now it so happened that the burning car was right under our bedroom, so you can be sure that I very gingerly sprinted around those premises to get the necessary items of clothing. I then headed down to the bedroom that was farthest away, all thoughts of the manuscript pushed out by the urgency of the moment.

"Glad the kids are in school," I mumbled as I pulled myself together. "With their kick for excitement, they'd probably be down there *fanning* it!" Still muttering, I made my way into my panty hose. (Would someone please tell me why anyone in their right mind would wear a pair of panty hose to their own fire?) About midway through the endeavor, I remembered the manuscript. Awkwardly, I made my way to the nearest window and hollered, "Gene! The manuscript—" and just then the firemen doused the car with foam from top to bottom. I was heartsick, but Gene took the time out to tell me that a fireman had thrown it in the snow just before they doused the car.

Somewhat relieved, but still apprehensive, I (fully clad, finally) made my way to the front yard amid the neighbors, hoses, and fire engines, to a forlorn little package that was a bit wet, with black fuzzies all over it. I brushed the black fuzzies off, sniffed it and thought it smelled a bit scorched, but decided, *oh, well, maybe they'll just think it was a really hot manuscript,* and took it to the post office myself to get away from all the confusion . . . and promptly got busy on something else as the manuscript became a part of the English scene.

But within a few months, being basically nosey the way I am, I found I had all kinds of questions. Calling England at the drop of a pound wasn't practical, so I called the joint publishing company here in the states . . . only to find that they'd severed all ties with England due to—you guessed it—the drop of the pound. Well there I sat with questions unanswered, and a sinking feeling that something had gone wrong.

After much prayer and nailbiting, I called England and asked them to release me from my contract. And they most graciously did, understanding my dilemma and problems attending. However, somehow it never got put into writing. A verbal release was comforting, but would never stand up in a court of law. But they assured me that they'd mailed the original manuscript, plus the contract, so I had only to wait . . . and wait . . . and wait. Well, the original manuscript never did arrive back here. But fortunately, they (England) had sent a xeroxed copy to Logos International as one last attempt to get an American company to go with them on this venture. Logos was notified about the release of contract, and that put my manuscript into another "category" of consideration, so as I patiently waited for written release, I also waited for word from Logos regarding the manuscript as being considered for this country.

Many moons went by. And several sailing vessels came to and fro, but none bearing me a manuscript. Then, one day while jogging-in-place to the tune of falling plaster and quaking china, I decided I should call Logos to see what had become of one yellowed, faded manuscript. Neither Vi nor Dan Malachuk were in. Later that day, Vi called me. "Char, do I ever have a story to tell you. You see, your manuscript was originally rejected"—enter heart palpitations and cold sweats—"but we didn't have any address to send it to! And since your call this morning, someone else has been poring over the manscript and feels that perhaps we should reconsider—what I'm saying Char, is that 'that which was dead is alive again!' " And with that comment, the blood started to flow in my veins again. Why had God held that manuscript up? Why did Satan try to burn it? Why was it rejected and then no address? Why? Because God is the Blessed Controller of all things. (Someone suggested that God was waiting for a violent winter where everyone would be so "snowed in," they'd read *any*thing!)

24

The letter I held in my hand had a brisk but friendly tone to it. "We of the 700 Club would like to have you appear on our program. Could you make arrangements?"

Could I! The possibility shot 700 buckets of adrenalin into my veins as turbulent thoughts tumbled out of the cobwebs in my brain. *Lose twenty pounds? No—not enough time . . . suggest they use a wide-lense camera . . . I'll try to smile primly, or my eyes will look closed all the time . . . what shall I do about my glasses? Don says I look like Adam Ant in them . . . maybe I shouldn't wear them . . . but if I don't, I'm sure to walk right into the drum set . . . need time with the Lord . . . check schedule . . . House guests for two weeks . . . Lay Witness team staying over weekend . . . neighbor going in for surgery . . . and a speaking engagement . . . file quiet times under "less sleeping time."*

Break news to family. "You'll never guess what happened to me on my way back from the mailbox," I whinnied.

"Something great, I hope—is that vegetable soup I smell?" sniffed Gene.

Laurie: "Mom, should I put my hair in a bun, or just let it hang straight for that wedding Saturday?"

"Any way, but not in my soup or *my* bun," I sighed as I

plucked a thirty-foot hair from the counter top.

Mark: "Mom, dad said I could get a dune buggy—I got my own money, y'know. . . ."

Jamie: "Hey, you guys wanta' see my imitation of a water sprinkler again—isssssssk-chee-chee-chee—ft-t-t-t—It's gettin' better, isn't it?"

Quietly, I patted the letter in my sweater pocket as I dreamily—and sloppily—ladled out the soup. As the steam rose from the dutch oven, I saw visions of myself genteelly saying "no" to Phil Donahue, Johnny Car. . . .

"Char, you just set the ladle in the butter. Are you okay?" from my hungry husband.

Day of arrival. Posh hotel. Carpets so thick, I needed snowshoes. Great service. Super sleep in spite of the flashing red neon sign that splashed "Sha-zam" intermittently throughout the night sky.

Big morning. I sat quaking in the hotel lobby looking like a "Palpitating Plum" in the purple "comfy" long dress I'd chosen to wear, waiting to be picked up by Prince Charming in a 700 Club limousine. Down the luxurious corridor, I caught sight of two lovely creatures lounging around the lobby. One wore a gorgeous wool shawl thrown casually around her shoulders. I sucked in my breath and said, "Wow. Now Lord, that's what an author should look like," as I rearranged the purple plumage on my lap. Characteristically, I knew that if *I'd* dared to throw an ecru-colored shawl around me that way, all the hotel help would be asking, "When did you *break* your arm?"

My reverie was broken by the arrival of Prince Charming. And he was. Charming, I mean. And a prince of a fella' too, as his Father was indeed a king!

I conjured up what I thought would be a look of elegance

befitting the occasion as I glided along the immense corridor on his arm, but sounding more like a prattling Purple Plum, with several "hee-hee's" and "ahhhh-ha ha's" thrown in for nervous release. Just as we made our way through two huge glass doors, the two gorgeous creatures confronted us. In a sultry voice, and with a graceful hand extended toward me, one of the creatures smiled and said, "Hello . . . I'm Joyce Landorf . . . we're sharing the show today. . . ."

"Joyce *who?*" I blabbered. I'd heard her plainly enough, but I just needed a moment to catch my composure. From a far distance, I heard someone explaining that the other lovely was her P.R. agent from Revell. I decided I had to contain my excitement and act as though being thrust into the midst of celebrities was a normal way of life for me. I don't think I had them fooled for even a moment. I'd managed to add "heh-heh's" to my broadening vocabulary of nervous reactions, with "ahems" threaded throughout the conversation.

Finally, it was make-up time. Twitteringly, I told the make-up man not to fill in my dimples as they were the only thing I had going for me. Fortunately, he didn't hear me.

Curtain time. The Palpitating Plum perspiring up to point of paralysis, propped and prepped by prop man! By some mystical force, I found myself shaking hands with Pat Robertson and somewhere from my depths, dredging up a reasonable facsimile of grace and composure. I'm not sure it wasn't a bit hypocritical, as actually, I wanted to kick him in the shins and hiss, "How would *you* like to be twenty pounds overweight and follow Joyce Landorf?"

Interview over. Prop men busy spooning up this huge mound of Purple Plum jelly. . . .

25

Wonderingly, I the author ask myself why you, the faithful reader, have even felt led to read my book this far . . . was it the hint of housewifely humor? The chance of escape into the life and trials of another? Curiosity, maybe? Or was it—could it be, oh, merciful and caring Father, an aura that surrounds it—an essence of the Holy Spirit—something that speaks of reality, of honesty? Oh, I hope it *is* this!

For I'm convinced that people are sick to death of fairy tales, myths, half-truths, masks, cover-ups, and shallowness. The human heart of today that succumbs so easily to heart disease is also the heart that longs for sharing, transparency, integrity, and will search anywhere, go to any lengths, to find fulfillment.

Recently, I received this letter from a young housewife in Texas. She said, "I was raised in a Christian home but left God (had I ever really found Him?) as a teenager. It went from bad to worse after I married and I eventually ended up on the verge of losing my husband, baby boy, and the respect of my very respectable parents. Why? The age-old quest . . . looking for "love" and "fulfillment" everywhere except from the only true source of those two things.

"Well, apparently some of my 'churchianity' stuck

because one day I found myself standing in front of a Christian book stand in a Piggly Wiggly Supermarket praying 'God, if you're up there and you really care about me, you'd better lead me to a book that will lead me back to *you* 'cause it's almost too late.' "

I'll take just a moment here to squeeze through the extreme pleasure it gives me when I tell you that He led her to my first book and that, yes, it was the "link" as she calls it, that restored her to fellowship with her Savior, and while I'm picking bits of hay and stubble out of my mouth—(vainglory can be *so* prickly!) I want to make a point.

That: Our hearts are starving for real and honest relationships, but the fear and pain that is involved in establishing these relationships is so unbearable, we take an easier route by seeking to read about some first, hoping we will find a quicker, more palatable remedy. And I'm just as bad off as you are, because I can be more honest with you here than I can be with my own family over the dinner table. But again, you don't interrupt as much as they do, either.

If you and I were sitting over my chipped coffee cups, I'd be aware of the plainness of my face, the fear that I might be a terrible disappointment to you, the clock that's always pressuring, the demands of schedules (but I'd never want you to *know* this) that try to rule us. And you'd forget to think of me as a housewife who struggles with sagging souffles and broken zippers. You'd think in terms of author/speaker/ general-do-gooder—although you'd never want *me* to *know* this.

Like yesterday, I heard of a young housewife who desperately needs some counsel, but won't come to me—though she wants to—because she "feels inadequate" in my presence. How can I tell her that because of that very thing. . . because she thinks of herself as the very "least" of the brethren, she can come to me *as Christ*? For if she would give me the privilege of giving her but a small drink of water—some tiny bit of comfort, something to slake her thirst, it would be the same as doing it to Christ.

But she and I will not be able to really come together until we come before Him. Humbly, brokenly, asking forgiveness for my having given false impressions of busy-ness and pretension, and she, for not sensing her uniqueness and importance in the body of Christ. But having stepped into the light as He is in the light, we can have fellowship, one with another. Not as one who is thought of as "adequate" counseling from a higher level, *down to* one who feels "inadequate" but as two equal sinners "standing in the need of grace."

But of the two kinds of sharing, one to one, or this other artless method of draping my heart over the typewriter, I think I like this "keyed up" one the best. I can share the "inside me" without concerning myself with what you think about the outside me . . . the lumpy, ego-starved, self-conscious me. The me that gapes in wonder to think that another could feel inadequate before me when my own insecurities are screaming so loudly!

26

Home. Such a warm sounding word. On a scale from one to ten, I'd say ours would rate about a three with *Better Homes and Gardens.* But you must realize that *Better Homes and Gardens* doesn't approach life realistically. If only they'd include a few glass-rings on their table tops . . . at least one authentic smear of grape jam under every light switch . . . complete with one summer sandal peeking from under the sofa . . . a paper plate with a partial, dried hamburger bun and a sentinel Pepsi bottle standing at attention beside the T.V. Then women could enthusiastically declare, "Yes, *yes!* I *could* incorporate all this into my decor!"

Yes, home . . . place of refuge . . . and refuse. The most recent thing has been the 200 beer cans that Jamie managed to sell for 97¢. The next thing for him is striking it big with his pet rock collection. (He thinks they are going to reproduce.)

But home really means so much to me. In fact, I get homesick just grocery shopping. And when I have to leave for speaking engagements, spasms of distress envelop me even before I've pulled out of the driveway!

One of the reasons I'm so satisfied here, is because God found this home for us. From our former, smaller home Gene and I had gone round and round with my "but I *need* a larger home" and his "but I *like* it here" until we were talked—and cried—out. Finally, one day I said, "Lord, this thing is up to you. Gene says that if he *ever* moves, which he doesn't seem to ever want to do, that it will have to be a large home in a nice district, plenty of shade trees, and available for a good price. In the meantime, I rest my case. Forever, if you choose."

Six months went by. One night, Gene walked in and said, "I saw a house over on the north side of town we might like to look at . . . let's take a run by it right now."

I rather disinterestedly put my coat on, as actually, I'd liked to have finished the T.V. program I was watching. So I halfheartedly mumbled, "Where is it located?" as I slo-o-o-wly buttoned my coat, eyes glued to the T.V.

"It's on Greenleaf."

"Oh." With about as much expression as you would get from one who didn't even hear you and who was secretly wishing she was capable of writing scripts like the one she'd been watching—*almost* to the conclusion.

But in the car, I spluttered "*Greenleaf!* Gene, that's where wealthy people live! We couldn't . . . it's not us . . . I'd never feel comfortable there," I ended up, feebly. Wasn't he aware of some of the hurts I'd had to endure from some of those kids from "the other side of the tracks"? Oh, some had been kind . . . but some had been cruelly snobbish, and so . . . so *condescending!* I remained quiet as we drove by a stark, barn-like structure, barely able to trace its silhouette because of a sparse moon.

But the next morning, Gene called the real estate man, and we went off to see Gene's "find." He'd already braced me by saying, "Now Char, when you see it in daylight, I want you to realize it needs a bit of work . . . paint is a little chipped. . . ."

Chipped! It was blistered, peeling, flaked and swaying in the breezes! Every *board* had rebelled! This? On Greenleaf?

It looked as though it should have been condemned! But once we were inside, we found that the outside looked great—in comparison!

Gene's most elaborate comment was, "Hm-m—m, " as the salesman kept up his glowing report of its possibilities. Meanwhile, I was eyeing the huge puddle-spots remaining from the Great Dane that ruled the house previously. (Granted, I'm not sure I would have stood at the door and argued with something that big, either.) As I flicked bits of plaster out of my hair from the recently caved-in ceiling, I noticed that the light fixtures were loosely archaic, but mostly broken. The bedrooms were aflame with psychedelic paper. The whole ridiculous mess had a high price attached to it, and more than likely, high tax rates besides. Hardly looked like something my economical, conservative husband would ever consider and I was glad, because the house not only depressed, but frightened and overwhelmed me.

The next morning, as Gene was getting ready for work, he gurgled, "Have you thought" (splat) "any more about that" (pa-tooey) "house we looked at yesterday?" as he finished brushing his teeth.

I took a deep breath and said, "Well, I . . ." only to realize that he'd plugged his electric razor in, so I turned to the nearest lampshade in my bedroom and proceeded to reiterate all of my dislikes about that impossible house we'd seen. Lampshades in our house are always cocked at a rakish angle that gives them a compassionate attitude, so when Gene finished shaving I hardly felt it was all worth repeating to him. I felt the lampshade and I had shed enough light on the situation.

But I got just a little squeamish when I heard Gene call the real estate man and tell him he'd take it if they'd come down five thousand dollars. I decided that men were like little boys playing Monopoly, so I took the kids and went off shopping. I came home feeling a little piqued as I couldn't find what I needed and would have to go into an adjacent town. It didn't help matters any when I walked into my house—my tiny, oft-complained-about house—to find Gene and the real estate man at the table with reams of important-looking papers spread out before them. Gene looked a bit sheepish and grinned, "Hope you liked it at least a little bit—because we just bought it."

And quietly within, somewhere between the nausea and my heart, I heard a voice reminding me—"a large home in a nice district, plenty of shade trees . . . at a good price."

Well, there I was, a proud homeowner of a dilapidated mess in a snooty section, complete with high taxes and crabgrass. The crowning blow came when I continued shopping. Mark, who was seven at the time, kept pulling his T-shirt down around his hips. I complained, "Why are you doing that?" He retorted with, "Cuz I can't keep my zipper shut!" and when I pulled off Jamie's boots in the shoe store, he had on one red and one blue sock! I fumed, "Some big homeowners we are turning out to be! Kids look like we are on welfare!"

But God wasn't upset by my poutiness. He directed me in the decorating, pointing me to decisions that were to fill me with gratitude continually, for these decisions resulted in easy care and upkeep. And guess what! People love to come to my house—referring to it as warm and homey—peaceful and comfortable. To me, it is a little corner of heaven! And because God found it for us, it just gets homier and nicer all the time.

27

I have often said that I was a chapter going somewhere to happen. No longer do I feel like that. Now I know that I am a chapter just sitting around home, while happening. Take last Monday, for instance. I'd gotten up early, which isn't all that newsworthy, but without those moments with the Lord, I'm sure I'd never have made it through the day as graciously—give or take a little—as I did.

Jamie started the day off royally by defying my authority. Have you ever stepped out of the shower and made the discovery that your youngest needs a wallop, and one just can't run down the stairs and out into the yard in that condition to wallop? So I put on my clothes hurriedly enough so that most things were inside out and funny-buttoned, but when about to throttle a gang of kids in your own backyard, style is not imperative.

As I sailed down the stairs, I discovered one of the dear ladies from our church sitting on a kitchen stool, quietly waiting for a gracious cup of coffee, so I patted her on the head and assured her that I would come in and be sweet to her, just as soon as I mopped up the neighborhood with a few kids.

After the verbal slaughter, my nerve ends were just

receding nicely when my teenage friend Chuck arrived. His mother's third marriage wasn't doing too well, and he was really down. As he pulled out of the driveway to go to work, my friend Katie pulled into the driveway. She and I had spent some time together a few days prior to this, and during this time, she'd tried to convince me that she was a jinx—that bad things always happened when she was around. Of course I told her this wasn't true and we prayed against such an attitude.

She'd come to take Virgean to visit some nursing homes and as we approached Virgean's room, we could hear her muttering, "They are gone. I just know they are gone, lost!"

"Virgean, what's lost?"

"The drawers to my filing cabinet . . . they were here when I shipped this stuff, but now they are gone."

"Honey, you had this thing taped up like a tomb! The drawers *couldn't* be gone! Let's see . . ." and I began to feel around. "Virgean, you had it upside down, with TOP marked on the bottom . . . that's all!" And she very sheepishly joined us in our laughter. After we'd chatted awhile and helped Virgean unpack, there was another knock at the door.

It was Chuck back again, with a face longer than the latest hemlines.

"Char, I just got fired." When you are seventeen, it can almost seem like the end of the world. Or any other age, for that matter. Although I didn't know what to say to him, I weakly invited him in just as Katie and Virgean were leaving. About five minutes later, a discouraged Katie stuck her head around the front door. "Char, you'd better come out here . . . I just backed into Chuck's car." I shook off the "they say I'm a jinx" bit that kept trying to squeeze up into my consciousness and made soft clucking sounds, the kind you are supposed to make when you feel entirely helpless but want to be consoling.

Jamie, having worked his way back into my good graces, appeared on the scene, jumped back dramatically when he saw the caved-in car and yelled, "Wow! Chuck! We can paint big numbers on the side and race it this weekend." The laughter helped to relieve the tension of the moment, but not the problem. Katie had no insurance and Chuck had no job and I had no solutions.

I had to go off to an appointment, so I left the house. When I returned, someone had left a newly purchased gallon of ice cream out to melt all over the counter top. And when I sent Jamie down the stairs to get something out of the freezer, he bellowed from the bowels of the basement, "Moth-h-her! Someone left the freezer door open and everything is spoil-l-led!" It just all seemed to cap off a lovely day. Nerve ends were gasping from soaring adrenalin and mounting blood pressure. But life, when involved with others, becomes complex yet blessed. Most of this would not have happened as a part of my life if we had not committed ourselves to a fellowship. Yes, I could have spent more time in sitting around in isolation—and boredom. But as their hurts become my hurts, as their problems become my problems, the Savior of love prays for them through me. He, who is a man of sorrows and acquainted with grief, intercedes for them as only a God of love can. But this same man who lives within is also the Spirit of joy and rejoicing. He, the great burden-bearer, is also the great joy-giver. Because of this, we can smile through our tears, laugh away our hurts and sing in the face of adversity.

But, when I pulled the covers up around both of my chins that night, I was reminded of the old Presbyterian who said, "Whew, I'm glad that's over," after he'd fallen down a flight of stairs. I was happy to be one day closer to the coming of the Lord, and happy to have that particular Monday behind me as past history.

28

Pleasant atmosphere . . . china clinking, quiet conversations pulsing around us. As the waitress brought our order, I couldn't help noticing that my friend Bea looked a bit strained.

"Char, I haven't been sleeping too well. I spend much of my time in tears . . . it's my husband's job. He doesn't know whether to quit this job and go into another field . . . and I don't know what kind of direction to give him . . . I'm really churned up over the whole thing."

"Bea, honey . . . relax. You don't really have to give him *any* direction. God hasn't called you to that. You are to give him support, encouragement, trust, and lots and lots of warm sexual love . . . and just trust God for the decisions your husband will make . . . much better, and more quickly, with*out* your help. You don't want to become his mother-image, do you?" While I was talking I was pouring the syrup on my French toast.

The waitress came along and chirped, "Here is your syrup . . . 'scuse the delay."

I looked at Bea, then at the waitress, "Then whatever did I just pour?"

The waitress gave me a blank stare, "Uh—your Sanka

coffee, m'am." I knew she was stifling a smirk, and I couldn't blame her . . . we were laughing our heads off, so much so that we managed to attract the attention of everyone in the restaurant, but the delay was good for a longer period of sharing. Settling back into the conversation again took a bit of restraint, but we did it.

"Bea, I have a favorite prayer. It is this: 'Oh, Lord . . . a roof over my head, food on the table, a few clothes for my back . . . and an occasional trip to Europe . . . that's all I need, Lord."

With that, she managed to spill most of her coffee all over *her* breakfast! "Gleaning wisdom from you," she muttered as she wiped her hands on her napkin, "is about as meaningful as approaching the mannequin in the fun house that laughs all the time." But her eyes were smiling, and I think all the laughter was helping to rid her of some of her tension.

"Sorry, Bea . . . I don't mean to seem as though I'm taking it lightly. But I'm just trying to help you get your thoughts sorted out. If your trust is in God, as I believe it is, then He will see to all your needs. As you pray and seek God, you can know and be assured that He will give your husband the direction *he* needs."

The waitress—still smirking—had begun to clear our table off. I then found out why you should never put your elbows on the table. I was left facing a puddle of syrup, and several indiscriminate coffee blobs.

"But Char, won't that make me some kind of a doormat?"

"No," I said. "That doesn't mean that you can't share your feelings and your fears with your husband . . . but as you share them, always convey that you trust his judgment and will stand wholeheartedly behind his decision. If your heart attitude is right as you share with him, it will not build up that 'resistance' that can creep into a relationship so quickly.

84

When that starts building up, oftentimes it makes a man want to do just the opposite of what his wife desires, just to prove to himself that he is still boss. Their right to leadership is precious to them . . . and when we start getting pushy an alarm goes off inside of them. They feel the urge to protect their rights."

The waitress stood a short distance away, making strange guttural sounds in her throat. "Bea, I think they want to clear this table . . . probably want to run it through a car wash . . . we'd better leave."

As I left the tip, I managed to spill my water. "Good for the coffee stains," I stammered to the waitress as I walked out.

29

Oh, no! I sighed impatiently, as I slumped down into the seat behind the steering wheel. I was caught in an alley behind the courthouse, impossibly wedged in between two telephone trucks. The two men manning the trucks seemed to be enjoying my dilemma. "Have you out in a minute, lady . . . soon's we get done here." Oh, well. At least they weren't snarling at me.

Lord, I'll do my best not to fume. You know I have to catch a flight, plus finish packing. Seems like such a waste, just to sit here . . . wish I had a book to read . . . my thoughts were interrupted by some commotion behind the courthouse.

Officers were putting three youths, wrists and ankles chained, into a police car. I studied those young faces. I was witnessing a real life drama, and the reality of it all gripped me.

Father, those boys are barely more than children. I know these policemen are doing what you've called them to do in their capacity of upholding the law. I know they have to step in where the church has failed, but those boys don't look like hardened criminals to me . . . their parents, Lord . . . are they caring, even now? Oh, God, how they must be suffering. Parental failure . . . who hasn't felt its sting at one time or another?

I was suddenly aware that tears were streaming down my face. I wasn't even sure I could see to drive, as the puzzled telephone men waved me on ... I'd probably heaped mounds of guilt on them as they saw my tears, thinking they'd upset me. But my tears were as much for my own children, as for those boys and their parents. I couldn't wait to get home to tell the kids how much I loved them. I wondered, had anyone recently told those boys in that police car that they loved them? Whatever crime they'd committed—had it been a ploy for attention?

Lord, thank you for holding me up in that alley—those boys need a touch from you, Lord. I'm just naive enough to think that you put me in that place at that time so I would pray for them. And to help me see the importance of showering my own children with love . . . your love, Lord. Thank you.

30

Sometimes, people expect false humility. I've had people come up to me and say, "Oh, I loved your book so much! It was tremendous."

But when I come back with a pleasant, "Thank you—I enjoyed it immensely, too!" I get a puzzled expression in return for my honesty. I laughingly put my arm around them and say, "But don't stop loving me *now!* It's just that nothing I write can ever bless you if it hasn't first blessed me . . . nothing I've written will ever make you smile, if it hasn't made *me* smile first."

And darling, come now . . . let us reason together. If I didn't think, secretly, that my books were "good" I'd never have attempted to get them published!

But you see, God has given me a precious treasure. It is the gift of communicating, and I hug it to me, and embrace it as very valuable. And it's my very own! It's a part of the uniqueness God has given me. It's mine to use, however I wish.

I've chosen, by an act of my will, to use it for His glory. But it would have been no less my gift, had I chosen to write pornography, or to use it *against* Him. His love is so free, He leaves the choice to us.

There is a proverb that says that "your gift will bring you before great men." You and I know that the Word tells us that the very "least" of the saints is greater than even John the Baptist. So if you are really down on yourself about now . . . feeling the weight of your sin . . . and not making much spiritual progress, at least in your own eyes, I want you to know something. You may think of yourself as the very "least" of the saints, but in my book (literal translation permitted) you are the very "great ones" that my precious gift is bringing me "before."

And so, your highness—I come "before" you. I come bearing the gift of communication—the gift of sharing my heart. You see, my Father is a king, and He wants you to know of His deep love. He wants you to know that He is listening for your faintest whisper, the very slightest move you might make toward Him. He has said, "Draw nigh to me, and I will draw nigh to thee." He has forgiven you of all—*all* your sins—even the silly inconsequential ones you are worrying about right now, and he has made you "kings and priests."

And if it hadn't been for this "gift" of writing He's given me, I couldn't have had my heart draped over that bookrack, that book table, that bookshelf . . . even that trash can . . . wherever you happened to pick this up from, to read.

Truly, my gift has brought me before great men. . . .

31

A women's retreat . . . the only place I know where I can shower, then wipe with a towel that smells as though someone has dried walnuts in it.

So many things can happen at a women's retreat. I've known times when the anointing of God was so heavy, I could quote nursery rhymes and God would bless . . . my children have said, "Oh, mom . . . you wouldn't!" To which I cock my head knowingly to one side and squeal, "Mar-y had a lit-tle lamb . . . his name was Jesus!" Then, if no one I'm trying to impress is looking, I stick out my tongue at them.

But back to women's retreats . . . where my children aren't. Which just could be something in favor of retreats after a day like today.

I'd been ministering with what I thought was great freedom. It seemed to me as though the whole camp had come alive with a contagious vibrancy. There almost seemed to be a crackle in the air—a warmth, a glow.

The next morning, during what few moments I could snatch alone, I heard a tap at my door. When something raps that softly at your door at a women's retreat you don't knock yourself out getting there. It might be something furry . . . and hungry. But with the second light rap, I decided this whatever-it-was would greet me at least at eye level, so I answered the knock. An older woman, sad-faced and rigid, stood before me. Stoic, and silent. Something needed to be said by someone, so I said, "Yes?"

"Are you Charlene Potterbaum?" she queried.

"Yes, would you like to come in?" Evidently she didn't like to as she made no move. Just stood there, first on one squeaking board, and then another. Atmosphere? Awkward.

"Uh . . . is there anything I can do for you?" I tried, once more.

"No . . . no, I guess not. I was just wonderin' though . . . well, I was at the meeting last night . . . say, is that all we can expect today? More of the same? I mean . . . I was told this wasn't going to be just another women's meeting . . . I was looking for some depth. . . ."

Horror of horrors . . . I wanted to *giggle!*

"Please, won't you come in." She did. Cautiously. "Here, sit on the bed. I'm truly sorry you were disappointed. But I refuse to be under any condemnation. God called me to speak at this retreat and He uses me where I'm at, spiritually. The responsibility of each meeting is His, not mine. If the meeting goes well, He gets the glory, but likewise He absorbs the blame if it *doesn't* go well—and it pretty well leaves me scot-free to just be myself. I'm sorry if you weren't blessed. As to whether or not it was 'just another women's meeting,' I can only say that when you get two hundred women assembled together under the same roof, more than likely . . . you are going to have a women's meeting."

None of this seemed to move her. She asked to pray for me, and I prayed for her. I felt such sorrow for her. So joyless, so bound.

But I was happy to see that I was growing up. An incident like this would have crippled me a few years ago. Now I could fold it up and tuck it away among my memoirs . . . with the towel that smelled like someone had dried walnuts in it.

91

32

Yes, women's retreats are memorable occasions. Once when I was co-speaking with a precious bit of dynamite we'll call Sal simply because it wouldn't be helpful to anyone to know her real name, I was given some tremendous insights into human nature.

From the time I met Sal, I loved her fervently. There was something so powerful about her ministry, so heartwarming. Her radiant face, charming feminine giggle, her unique expressions, wit, plus the godly authority she had made a deep impression upon me. As I observed her, I couldn't help but think that she must have been raised in a strong Christian home that was oozing with Christian love and care.

We were about to wind up the retreat when God just kind of moved in and did His thing, the way only God can. Suddenly, confessions were spilling out and great cleansing was taking place. As Sal and I were praying for first this one and that, a young woman came up to us. She stammered a bit at first, but finally made herself clear. "That prayer you prayed, about us having no condemnation. . . oh, I need so to be freed from that. I hate myself so. . . can you help me?" And her tears began to flow.

Brokenly, she began to unmask herself.

"You see, as a young girl, I was raped by my brother and I've never been able to get over it. I've had hours of counseling . . . years of confusion. I was removed from my home and put into a home with an older sister with a deep-seated hatred for men. She told me constantly that I'd never get over it, and that I'd never have a normal sex relationship, ever."

Quietly, Sal took her hands. She said, "My being here is no accident. You see, I, too, was raped by a relative at a very tender age. Several times, in fact. I, too, was put into the home of a relative with deep problems. All of this led into great uncleanness for me, until I was certain that my only hope of escape was suicide. But God had different plans for me."

I felt as though I was watching from a great distance, almost as though God was allowing me to sit in on this conversation, yet not to be a part of it. This was strictly for these two who had suffered in much the same way.

As Sal and this dear girl were praying, again I felt as though God was allowing me this bit of drama for His own reasons, when abruptly, in the middle of praying, Sal blurted out, "Tell me . . . does your guilt and loathing stem from the fact that you know deep in your heart that you encouraged this act . . . may even have *enjoyed* it?"

A long, low, pitiful moan came from the distraught girl . . . a moan that was Spirit-inspired and bondage-freeing. "Oh, God! . . . God, Yes-s-s-!" And when that confession that had so needed to surface for so many years came forth, she was set free. She could face squarely now that it hadn't been rape—it was incest. She was willing to admit to her part in it, and be cleansed.

I wonder if I hadn't been permitted to be a part of that little tableau for just this reason . . . to share it with you. (I got their permission to use the incident, hoping it might help others.) But as it all took place, I couldn't help thinking of the verse that says, "She that has been forgiven of much, loves much," for Sal deeply loved her Savior. Every fiber of her being showed it. The forgiveness of God had made a radiant creature out of the one who walked in "uncleanness" before.

33

Grocery shopping and cooking are something I do only to keep my children from dying of malnutrition. If the time comes when I ever dwell alone, you may have to schedule I.V.s for me periodically, for I'm quite certain I will never darken the door of a supermarket again. Or at least not until dinner rolls around.

One day while grocery shopping, feeling smug and terribly clever because I'd managed to make it out the door without my penny-conscious husband and my computer-brained son, both of whom nearly drive me to distraction by figuring out prices per ounce, which toilet tissue has the most footage, which jars have fake bottoms, which company is falsely advertising, what's on sale and what's for free! All I'm really after is a fairly well-balanced larder with just enough junk food thrown in to make it interesting.

As I was slow-w-w-ly pushing my cart around, a very small boy, I'd say about age eight, passed me. We smiled. We passed again, next aisle. I noticed that he had a newspaper clipping circled. Grocery specials, no doubt. We smiled again. I said "Do you need any help?"

"Yeah, this special on paper toweling, I can't reach it . . . would you, please?" I placed the bargain in his basket, thanking him. I wasn't aware of the bargain myself.

He went back to studying his list and newspaper clipping intently.

My anointed nosiness began to run. "Is your mother here in the store somewhere? You seem to be awfully young to be doing the shopping."

"No, I'm doing it by myself," he proudly announced. "My dad'll pick me up." He squinted at his list again. "Say, can you read my mother's writing? See, she's gonna have another baby any minute now. Guess the doctor said she shoulda' had it last week, and see, she cries a lot. She can hardly walk. We know she won't cry any more after the baby comes, cuz this is her fifth, and she always does this just before a baby comes,'specially if it doesn't come when the doctor says it's 'sposed to."

Hm-m-m. Yes, I know the feelings well, as a rush of memories hit me.

"Well, see, I'm the oldest," and it seemed as though he drew himself up an inch or so as he said it, "and I told my folks I could do this, an' . . . what did you say this word was?"

"Cleanser." By now, I'd turned my cart around and we found ourselves heading in the same direction. I asked him if he minded and he said no, that that would be fine. We looked for the cleanser but undauntedly, he said, "We have to have a certain ounce size . . . the one on sale, here in the paper."

Shades of a computer-brained son, I muttered.

"Hm-m? Whadcha say?"

"Shades from the sun—my sunglasses—just wondered if I dropped them," I lied.

Together, we shifted all the cans of cleanser around until we found the right size. He put it into his cart like a trophy. He was being such a blessing to me!

We were both draped awkwardly over the frozen foods bin

when I heard a strong cheerful voice behind us saying, "Hey, sport!" (I *hoped* he wasn't addressing *me*.) "How's it going?"

The little guy beamed proudly, "Got everything on mom's list, dad. This here lady only had to help me once or twice— and when I couldn't read mom's writing, she could. . . ."

The father gave his son a comradely hug, rumpled his hair and turned to me and said, "Thanks for your help. I didn't know how he'd do. He didn't want me to leave his mom. She really is miserable . . . did he tell you?" I nodded.

"I'm sure it can't be long now . . . thanks, again," he said. And the two of them walked out of my life. But not out of my heart. Suddenly, the supermarket wasn't so super any more . . . without my little friend.

Busy Saturday in a hardware store. Long line, end of day . . . tired check-out girls, harried customers. A small boy just ahead of me was clutching a bulging wrinkled bag in one hand, and his purchase in the other.

Finally, it's his turn to check out. I couldn't believe my eyes! Tenderly, he'd put his purchased treasure on the counter, and carefully extracted a *piggy bank* from his sack. Industriously, he began the process that we realized would go on for quite some time. Shake, shake . . . rattle, tinkle, clunk, shake. The checker looked dismayed, stammered and said, "Uh, this line's awfully long . . . better wait."

The little fellow's face fell. "But I have to get back. I left my little brother with the baby while she was sleeping so I could get here before you closed. I gotta get right back, but it's my mom's birthday, and we don't have no dad and I've saved a long time so I could get her this silverware. She's wanted it for so-o long."

People behind me started muttering, clearing throats. I had

the feeling he needed some encouragement.

"Hey, Tiger. . . we'll wait. Don't get upset." I ignored the scowl I got from the check-out girl and turned to the four behind me, all looking like stony impatience, personified. I felt a little nervous, but I turned to them and said with great bravado, "What if that was your son buying a gift for you? Would you be willing to wait?"

Sheepish grins. Downcast eyes. A spirit of comradeship came over us all. And as I was speaking, I heard a moan. . , the little guy was a dollar fifty-six cents short!

"But I *knowed* I had enough," he stammered, as little grubby pockets are being ransacked and wrong-sided. For his attempt, three more cents, a rusty key and a bubble gum wrapper were added to the pile of coins on the counter.

I turned, hoping I wouldn't be facing a lynch mob as I scrabbled around in my purse for some change. A big black man behind me caught my eye as he handed me a quarter. Silently, the others in the line reached into their pockets. I grinned, made up the balance, slapped the handful of coins triumphantly on the counter top and said, "Here! Paid in full! Now hurry home to that baby."

When I made my purchase, I turned to the faces behind me. Their expressions had been altered from indifference to a gentle softness. Strange, isn't it? Not one bit of Scripture had been quoted. Not one line of a sermon preached. But God met us there, that day in a hardware store. For you see, God is love and we felt Him there among us. I know those others felt Him, too.

34

Home from a meeting . . . bone-weary, frazzled but fulfilled.

"Lord, just before I drop off to sleep, let me say 'thank you' again. Let me say, just one more time, those precious words . . . I love you. Not just because you blessed the meeting . . . not because you watched over me so carefully, not because you gave me the gift of writing and women who will listen to me . . . no, I just want to say I love you, because you are you. Because you are God, and I need to express it.

"Lord, each meeting is so different. And I'm so awed when they ask me to be their speaker. So awed, when I remember the weak, whiney little creature I used to be . . . and even in my weakness and whining, in the midst of all that, I knew in my heart that someday I would be speaking before large groups of women. Yes, Lord, I've come a long, long way. I'm so glad, Father, that you don't wait until we are perfect to use us. Oh, I know that some of the whining has gone by the wayside. But the weaknesses you have exchanged for your strength, as you promised you would. And as I am becoming the kind of person I've always wanted to be, the 'me' that you had preordained me to be, I see that all the people around me are becoming the kind of people I've always wanted to have around me. Guess who's changed, Lord? I've got to get some sleep now. Please Father, take a moment to put your arms around that darling woman at the meeting who cried so because of her marriage . . . that precious one who put her arms around me and said, 'I start chemotherapy tomorrow . . . pray for me . . . I'm so frightened.' And that tired soul whose husband was so indifferent . . . let her know that you will be her husband . . . her comforter. The one whose daughter had just run away from home . . . give her peace. The little creature that said, 'I can't throw anything away . . . my house is a pig sty' . . . tell her she can throw things away, Lord. That in you, she really *can* do all things—oh, Lord, I feel so torn. I see them for such a tiny dot of time . . . our paths may never cross again, but I love them so . . . with your love, Lord. Mine would shrink and grow taut. But your love, your life—it flows on, unending, gracious, broad and satisfying . . . I'm really tired, Lord. But such a good kind of tired . . . the same kind of tired that caused you to sit by a well . . . sit by me, Lord . . . I'm going to sleep now. I love you."

35

I'd just come from a meeting that had been so free, but a startling thing had occurred after the meeting. I said, "Gene, I've never had such a thing happen before. This little cheery housewife bounced up to me and said, 'Oh, Char—you're such a riot! We are so much alike . . . tell me, what sign were you born under?' I was floored! I did what I could to explain to her that seeking after that kind of thing was 'spiritual adultery' but I had such a few minutes with her . . . so many people around wanting to share, and all . . . Gene, what should I do when they come to me with such a thing?"

He grinned. "Just tell them the sign you were born under . . . *Elkhart General Hospital* . . . that should do the trick." I sent my dishtowel crashing into his newspaper as I laughingly went to answer the jangling telephone.

As so often happens, a distraught housewife was on the other end of the line. She seemed to need some immediate attention so Gene encouraged me to meet her at the church, wisely noting that the din from the basement would hardly be conducive to thinking clearly as he shouted above the electric guitar, the blaring amplifier and the crashing cymbals.

So I met Darcy there in the quietness and seclusion of the church. And there, she poured out her heart. She confessed her faults to me, and I assured her that God would help her, and that he had already healed her of her faults. I was awed again, because of the tremendous responsibility that God has entrusted us with—that of being "kings and priests" to others, hearing their confessions. And I am not betraying her trust by sharing our time together, as I've gotten her permission, and I'm not using her real name.

Besides, her heart's cry is so universal, it could have been any number of you who are reading these pages even now.

Darcy had a good marriage, but a lonely one. She had found Christ, but her husband seemed to have no interest in the things of God. As is so often the case, she was torn between two allegiances.

I listened to her, then I prayed with her. After we'd prayed, she put her head on the table near me and wept.

"Darcy, God is cleansing you right now." I stroked the long hair, then brushed it from around her face. "He knows all about your hurt. He knows all about the pain you feel when you see couples that are in this thing together. He knows how you long to have your husband sharing this deep love for Christ you're experiencing. And Darcy, He even knows and understands that unexpressed feeling you have, that 'wishing' you'd married someone else. Would it make you feel better to know that many married people, in fact, I could almost say *all* married people feel that way at one time or another?

"Even Martin Luther had a grasp on this, for I just read something the other day where he said that our flesh is so corrupt and unsound that not even married people are free from illicit sexual desire. That if married people will examine their feelings carefully, they will discover that they like the form or manner of another more than they do their mate. That in everything, it happens this way—that what a man has, he despises; what he does not have, he loves."

She became very still. "How did you know?" she stammered.

I patted her arm. "Because there really is no new thing under the sun," I commented. "The struggle you are having in your thought life is the same battle that humans have tangled with since the Fall. But Darcy, this is the good news! God forgives you for those immoral thoughts. He died for that sin of coveting another's mate you are struggling with. None of us can keep the law. To be guilty in one point is to be guilty in all points. Have some of your thoughts been adulterous? That's okay, too, because Jesus took it all—He died for all of it, so that you might go free. But Darcy, there is another bit of great news I want to share with you. There is a way you can put all that sinful thought life to good use. Here's how."

She was busily blowing her nose and looking at me in amazement.

"Darcy, keep two fires burning in your heart. Allow one to be down in the left hand corner of your heart. Put all your sacrifices of praise on this altar. Every time an evil thought hits you, just say, 'Jesus, you died for that thought. That evil thought reminds me of what you've done for me, and I will never have to suffer, or stand before the wrath of God because of that evil thought. So I can praise you and thank you *for* that evil thought, because it reminds me again of your loving grace and forgiveness. I'll put it here on this altar as a sacrifice of praise to you.' "

She looked even more amazed, but kept saying "um-huh" as though she understood, so I went on. "On the other altar, you can pile up your offerings of praise. When you feel the stirrings of God's good graces within you, you can lift that as an *offering* of praise and put it on *that* altar. Then everything about you will be used to praise the Lord. Your goodness and your badness. Then it doesn't leave anything left over for the enemy to monkey with. He can't use your thought life against you, because every time he tries to condemn you with your awfulness, that very bit of awfulness will be that which will remind you of God's faithfulness."

"Is that what they mean about 'praising God in all things'?" she asked, as she shredded her Kleenex into a neat little pile.

"Yes, I guess you could say it is. I didn't realize I was being that profound. I just wanted to show you that you can put all your thought life to work for Jesus.

"Darcy! You look almost human again. Say, you haven't lived until you've watched me eat a chef's salad from a round-bottomed bowl . . . let's go eat someplace."

We closed up the church behind us and went away giggling like a couple of school girls. In my heart, I was wondering how anyone could ever tire of counseling people when God gives you such a fulfilled feeling, knowing that you are working in cooperation with the very God who created the universe. I've quoted it elsewhere, but it bears repeating, "If you get there the same time the Holy Spirit does, He'll make you look *real* good!"

36

Virgean came through the back door soaked to the bone, chilled, and very discouraged. I acted as though I hadn't noticed that she'd thrown down her backpack in disgust. I knew we were in for some kind of confrontation, so I just waited.

"I shouldn't have come here," she sobbed. "The town is too big . . . the motor on my bike still frightens me . . . it sounds too much like a motorcycle and it isn't working right . . . and—and all I could find was this stupid looking rain hat" and she put her head in her hands and cried some more.

I can't begin to tell you how helpless I feel when I see her suffering so. No one can tell her why God has called her to serve Him in this disabled body. But then again, she doesn't ask.

I just took one of her hands and let her verbalize some more. She seemed very much like a little girl as she wiped the tears from her face. "And . . . and I shouldn't be telling you all this. I should have just gone into my bedroom and cried out to God, like I used to back in Emporia."

"Virgean, I think that's why God sent you to us. You spent too much of your time with God, alone. You know, anyone can be spiritual, all by himself. But the going gets a bit rougher when you are forced to rub shoulders with people who aren't exactly like you, and expose your weaknesses for scrutiny. Besides, you get a little spooky."

"Spooky?" she sniffled.

"Yeah—spooky. Full of spiritual pride. Independence. A feeling that you are something special. You can come out all smiling and strong-appearing, but it can still come across almost as a spiritual phoniness. And if you go off into your little huddle with God, then isn't the eye saying to the ear, 'I have no need of thee'? Virgean, that little verse that says 'Confess your faults one to another, that ye may be healed' (James 5:16) was put there for a reason. We really do need one another."

"Wow. I forgot that was there." She was cleaning her nose so enthusiastically, I asked her if she needed the vacuum. The giggles released the discouragement, and we were soon hugging each other.

"But sometimes," she continued, meditatively, "I am uncertain as to my role. I think I can accept being single all my life, if that's what God wants for me . . . but there is such a deep down loneliness I feel."

"Honey, marriage won't necessarily relieve that entirely. That little tug of loneliness can be experienced by married people as well. That little ache you feel is the dissatisfaction God uses to call us to himself. It's a feeling of not being completely satisfied . . . because our true residency is in heaven, and we are only pilgrims and strangers here on earth. I think what we often mistake for loneliness could better be described as homesickness—for heaven. Perfection is the only thing that will take that feeling away, and we will only realize perfection when we stand in His presence, stripped of this sin nature that still clings like an oozing wound, even though we've been forgiven of all our sin."

She was drinking it all in, and I was thinking of the great joy it gives, to be pouring the living water from one needy vessel into another. And also, of how many times she'd tipped her overflowing vessel over into mine. "Virgean, when we try to project our thoughts into the future as to what might be, we'd be so much better off to just simply say, 'Thy will be done.' We should say it many times a day, when thoughts assail us and temptations nag at us. We need to draw ourselves up to the present moment and say, 'Thy will be done.' Thoughts wouldn't hold the power over us that we permit them to, sometimes.

"Now, why don't you be a dear girl and cook us some supper so I can go write a book. I'll let you throw wheat germ into anything you want to . . . except my coffee."

She got up, tottered for a moment, moved to the kitchen at her slow pace, saying dramatically, "Slo-o-o-owly, I turned . . ." and I was laughing when I headed off to my little chamber, to be alone with God . . . and get spooky, here with you.

37

Well, that moment is here. The moment when I should start writing. I've done all the preliminary things that writers do to postpone the moment of reckoning. I've dusted the table, rearranged my paper—three times. Put paper in machine, scratched my left elbow for two minutes, read all the labels on the cans peeking at me from the open pantry door, thought of a phone call that had to be made, stopped to examine a tear in the wallpaper and say "H-m-m-m."

I've rubbed the dog's tummy, stuck a cookie in my own, put in a load of wash, put a Band-Aid on my shin where I clobbered myself on the open dishwasher door. I peeled a patch of sunburn off my nose, I've sharpened every pencil in sight, I've examined a cupboard door hinge that seems to be loose, and remarked "Hm-m-m."

I put the load in the dryer, read the label on the soap box, ran to see what the dog was barking at, found out I was too late, and cleaned up the doggie-do. I've stared into space for eight minutes, I've chewed the inside corner of my mouth, I've pushed a basket of ironing out of sight so it couldn't scream "guilty!" I mourned over a broken fingernail and commented "Hm-m-m."

And now I know that I really must write. But I can't think of a thing to write about. But I am determined to write something, so I'll just wait a few minutes. And while I'm waiting, I'll dust the typing stand again, I'll rearrange my paper, I'll scratch. . . .

There really are days when I know I should have stayed with cookie-baking.

38

Ah-h-h-h. I had forty-five minutes free to work on my very special afghan. This afghan was very special to me, as it would prove to myself and to the rest of the world that not only was I a "spinner of yarns" but a crocheter of afghans, as well. For eons, now, I'd coveted the ability of other women who worked so nimbly with their fingers to create such masterpieces of warmth and cozy fireplace charm. I'd spent too long a time standing around "oohing" and "ah-h-hing" others as I would weakly say, "Uh—I write books, y'see."

But good ol' Proverbs 31 would begin to take root. I thought God would be pleased if I started draping some "tapestries" around our home, to set a more "grandmotherly" atmosphere for my babies to revel in.

So-o-o I learned, somewhat awkwardly, but determinedly, the art of crocheting. And one day, with sweating palms and fevered brow, I bought what is known in domestic circles as a "kit." I brought it home, nervously disengaged the huge box, reverently smoothing out the picture of the elegant creation on the front. That picture would be the "hope" my faith would rest on, for the eventual happening of that particular afghan in, I'd say, about the year two thousand, give or take a decade.

But when I opened the treasure, my first shock came when I found out that all the masses of yarn facing me had to be rolled into usable, manageable, loosely wound balls.

Well, there were some things that had to be attended to first. I knew I'd never enjoy working on said afghan if the house wasn't straightened, so I set about that bit first. Besides, I'd be baby-sitting Kari that afternoon, and that would be an ideal time to roll the yarn.

Oh, how grandmotherly, how homespun I felt as I cautiously began to roll that yarn. I dreamed, as I rolled, how thrilling it would be to cover my grandchildren with this prized heirloom I was going to make. And I was prattling all this to my precious little charge, Kari, who really couldn't have cared less, at age six months, squealing from her playpen in front of me.

"Lovey, when you grow up, grandma will wrap you in this ... and you can sit and memorize all of grandma's books." All the while, I was busy drinking up all her charm, when the yarn rolling came to a horrible, screeching halt! I'd been so busy admiring her and bragging about me that I didn't watch closely enough and when I glanced downward, I was faced with a matted, impossible tangle of yarn that had once been an important part of a very expensive afghan kit.

I picked the gurgling Kari up and buried my head in her delicious shoulder, moaning, "Comfort me, little one . . . tell me that an afghan isn't necessarily a part of grandmothering after all!" What a *mess!*

But then I realized that, like it or not, I was committed to that afghan. I didn't think that Gene, or even the Lord, for that matter would appreciate the wasted money, if it didn't materialize into something. So, thinking of how it would work patience in me, I began the arduous task of maneuvering my way through that mass of fuzz. I was chided, jeered, made fun of, guffawed at, but, undaunted, I continued, praising God all the way, because no trial lasts forever.

Well, that afghan and I settled down to a rather close relationship. It was to be three long off-white panels mysteriously crocheted together, with a wild smattering of violets thrown recklessly about. But every time someone saw the first panel they would always ask me if I was making thermal underwear. After the first violet made its appearance, however, they didn't ask any more. They just wondered.

But here I was, with forty-five minutes to spare. Great! But when I reached for the certain green that I needed, I was almost overcome with anger when I discovered that someone had taken my two greens that I needed, and more than likely, used them in a collage, or something. I was really burning!

Quietly, the Lord said, "You didn't know all that anger was down there, did you?"

I, seething still, said, "No, Lord! I didn't—but isn't anything sacred in this house? Don't I have any rights? I mean—"

"I thought you gave all your rights to me—didn't you?"

Calmer now, I muttered, "Yes . . . yes, Lord."

"And haven't I heard you tell others that people were more important than 'things'?"

"Yes, Lord . . . but where am I ever going to get thread to go with that which I've already used? How can I match it?"

"Have you forgotten that I, too, am a spinner of yarns? It's your anger we need to work on right now."

And quietly, the Spirit of the loving, living God began to bring gentleness back into my spirit. The afghan? Oh, it's a nice impressive looking lump in a basket by the fireplace. At least it gives the illusion that someone on the premises is domestic. When people glance at it, I grin and say, "Uh—I write books, y' see."

39

Gene has always been industrious. He is an avid businessman, and how I praise God for the way Gene has worked so hard to provide our needs—even managing to throw in some luxuries when my back was turned.

At one point in his business game, when he was the owner of a local appliance store, I asked, "Gene—there is one thing I need to know . . . when I die—will you close the store?"

He looked thoughtful for a moment, then replied, "Certainly. So long as you don't die on Saturday."

Now he has a manufacturing plant, and I think the hours are even worse. But he seems to thrive on the pressures that go along with business, so I accept his long hours as a fact of life and pray for him daily. There have been so many times when we've come to a screeching halt just short of bankruptcy—it could only have been God's caring intervention.

As the wife of a businessman, I've learned many valuable things. I've discovered that his business has to come first. As a young wife, I wanted so much to think that, as he pulled out of the driveway, his thoughts were of me, and me alone. Well, I've found out since, that if my face was before him, there was a ticker tape hanging from my mouth, and the

Dow-Jones report across my furrowed brow. By the time he rounds the corner, he has made a religion of the verse that reads, "Let those who have wives live as though they have none."

But it isn't all bad. By the time the frenzied business world has made him frazzled and out of sorts, he returns to this haven, where hopefully, a pleasant atmosphere has been established to be a balm to his jagged nerve ends.

I sometimes wonder if I express my appreciation well enough. Do I let him know how much it means to me that I don't have to get into that rat race and make part of the living? Do I thank him often enough for bearing up under strains I was never built for? Do I offer sympathy when the going gets rough? Do I complain, and make him feel guilty about the long hours? Oh, dear. I think I'm sorry I even started this chapter.

But this is the good news! He *forgives* me! He knows that he gave up his right to the perfect wife when he married me, so he just keeps on forgiving when I fail him, disappoint him, misunderstand him and don't say the things he needs to hear. He forgives, because God has asked him to . . . and he knows that God forgives me, too. When their forgiveness strums across this strung-up heart of mine, a song of joy wells up from within. Gene always says, "I've just learned to have a good forgetter."

40

I remember Laurie's promises. "Oh, Mom—when I get my driver's license, I'll do all your shopping, your errands, I'll take the boys wherever they need to go—just wait, you'll see."

Well, she'd gotten her license, and as usual, we were "hurrying" so she could go do her social climbing. I noticed that the telephone poles were winging by with unusual rapidity. She seemed intent at the wheel, so quietly I said, "Honey, did you see that sign back there? It said 'forty miles ahead.' "

"Sure, mom. I saw it. It said forty miles a head—that's forty miles for your head, and forty miles for. . ." and fortunately for us both, she had to come to a screeching halt for a light so we could giggle. (We are both accused of driving with our eyes shut while laughing.)

That was almost three years ago. Last night, she went gliding down a wedding aisle on her father's trembling arm. I was happy and content that she'd found her husband, Jay, but my heart was also very sad. I tried to cheer myself up by remembering that I hadn't really lost a daughter . . . I'd merely lost nine weekly loads of laundry . . . and gained a bathroom and telephone privileges.

As Gene and I stood in the back of the church, waiting for our turn to go down the aisle, we watched it fill up. . . and fill up. . . until Gene croaked, "What did she do? Run an ad in the paper? I thought this was supposed to be a small wedding! There's twice as many as expected!"

I patted him reassuringly on the arm, but I couldn't help thinking it would have been a great place to set up a book table. . . .

After the wedding we went through the usual exhausting clean-up details that go with such functions. My sister Lauraine said, "Let's go get a sandwich." My eyes looked like two glazed doughnuts, but I mumbled, "Yeah. Good idea."

At the restaurant, while they were intermittently picking rice from the folds of my dress and propping me back up in my chair, my sis asked me if I wasn't supposed to speak at a meeting somewhere in Michigan in the morning. "Yes-s-zzzzzz," I snored. She propped me up again and snapped her fingers in front of my face in order to resume the rather lopsided conversation.

"Is it an Aglow?" she asked.

Yawning, I replied, ". . . 'sposed to be. . . but the way I feel, I think it'll be just a li'l glimmer. . ." as I tried to curl up in her lap.

But as you can see, I lived to tell about it all. And that was the last daughter to be married off, so I'd like to think that any weddings we have left to endure will be less exhausting. But they all seem to have their own special blend of emotions, ranging from sad to glad, mellow to hilarious, touchy to tender, and, to hear Gene tell it, taking one from average wealth to instant poverty in about twenty minutes! But time goes on . . . the nest empties . . . and one generation makes standing room for the next . . . somehow, each wedding makes me feel a little older. . . and wiser. . . and chubbier.

116

41

Today my soul feels like brushed denim. Everyone who touches my heart seems to leave an impression. I don't know. Maybe it's just a rotten mood. And I don't think that moods can be prayed away. They must be resisted.

One of the recent soul-shreddings I've experienced had to do with a story that I wrote, intending it to be a gripping, dramatic, lesson-teaching incident, only to receive word from an editor that my masterpiece was not any of the above mentioned.

The pain was so excruciating, I had to chain my wrist to my typing stand to keep myself from running out to buy a consoling pound of chocolate.

Another shocker was discovering that someone had made reference to something I said in my first book, and then promptly went on to misunderstand me completely. Another shock wave came along when someone put my name in a book—with my permission—but when I found out the content of the book—too late, there was nothing I could do about it. Hazards of the profession, I think someone dubbed it.

Well, when my typewriter broke down, that did it! I bought the chocolate. Infantile, I know. Some regression back to the child-tape that says something sweet will make it all okay.

So I bought my favorites. The little lumpy package of Nestlé's tidbits in the brown package. Bought them as surreptitiously as any wino would his bottle—slipped them right into the grocery cart so the kids would think I needed them for baking.

Then, throwing restraint to the wind, I found a secluded corner and popped them pleasurably into my mouth, relishing each tiny morsel.

The doorbell rang. Caught. Strange, isn't it? How you don't feel guilty walking to the door with an apple in your hand, but you feel like a heel when you extend a sticky chocolate-y hand to someone? Well, I didn't know where I could hide the tidbits quickly so I put them out in full view on the kitchen counter top . . . but I put the flour sifter beside them as a decoy.

But it was only the paperboy. Back to my chocolates.

Eee-yuk-k-k. Chocolates now tasted like a brass doorknob. While washing my hands, I made a mental note. In fact, I thought the whole concept would look great in a fortune cookie. "He who fondle keys often, soon break chocolate habit."

I decided I would add this discovery to my growing list of "beat-the-sweets" suggestions. I now have five:

1. Inform entire family that last two pieces of candy in dish are yours.
2. Make all cookies very small. (Guilt experienced after three small cookies just as intense as guilt experienced after three large ones.)
3. Keep personalized toothbrush and paste in every room in the house, to quickly purge any whining tastebuds when you've had your little

fling.
4. Carry brass keys in your pockets to handle as brassy fingers retards hand-to-mouth tidbit popping.
5. Tell yourself that you are quite sure you saw a hair fall into whatever batter is tempting you.

You see, I was a total failure at one of these weight-reducing programs you go to. Besides, I rather like the verse that says, "They who put their trust in the Lord shall be made fat." And my Bible has a cross reference to that verse. It was, appropriately enough, "Godliness with contentment is great *gain*—" All the prophets of doom are proclaiming a famine in the near future anyhow—guess I'll just wait till then to diet. Besides, I read in a magazine somewhere that you could accomplish *anything* if you were willing to apply yourself to it for fifteen minutes a day. Great! I decided then and there to diet—just fifteen minutes a day!

42

When my brother was very ill with leukemia, someone in our community gave me twenty dollars to send to him in Florida. That night, my brother called me. I said, "Rog, I'll be sending the money to you."

Weakly, he said, "No, Char. My needs are being met, and we are doing fine. Keep that money in Elkhart, and help someone who is hurting there."

For a few days, I forgot about it. Then the Holy Spirit reminded me that I was to do something with that money. I called my friend Shirley who was working at the welfare department. I relayed Roger's message to her, feeling all warm and good in my heart because Roger had always had such a deep love and concern for this community. For twenty years, he'd been a policeman in this town and had delivered babies in the squad car (that were usually named after him), helped drunks to sober up, took in delinquents, saw to it that crippled children got to ball games, was Santa Claus every Christmas, made up like a clown for parades, and his crowning achievement was passing out huge parking "tickets" to children in the pediatrics ward. (The tickets had a place to make check marks if they "hadn't taken medicine," "snoring too loud," "sleeping with mouth open," etc. He was given an extended lunch hour to do this in.)

Shirley said that she had a very needy black family. The father was disabled. The mother had deserted them all, but a grandmother was helping him raise the children. When Shirley contacted the family, the grandmother wept as she said the children had no shoes, and school would be starting in one week.

Shirley, a fine Christian gal, told me later when we were talking: "Char, I did the strangest thing. I called our leading department store. My reason kept telling me that their shoes would cost more, but I kept thinking they were probably better quality.

"When I called and talked to the manager, alerting him that we would be coming in that afternoon, I nearly fell over when I heard him say, 'I'll leave word that our store will match that money.' When I arrived at the store with three black teenagers in tow, I found a friendly salesman ready to assist us. After going through what seemed like mounds of shoes, and gently encouraging the fourteen-year-old to consider practical shoes instead of some flashy ones he wanted, the salesman and I were dismayed to see that we'd overextended our cost by fourteen dollars.

"The salesman grinned, reached into his billfold as I got into my purse. We split the difference, the children had their shoes, and God had multiplied Roger's money from twenty dollars to fifty-four!"

Later, as Roger's illness progressed and bills really started soaring, this little community remembered all his love and devotion. When the discovery was made that they had no insurance, a fund was started in a bank downtown, and from all over the country, people started sending into that fund. They were people who'd been raised here but still kept tabs on things through the local paper. We were almost overwhelmed with the loving response of people. They gave to the tune of six thousand dollars! But God upholds his principles. *If you sow love, you are going to reap love.*

It was just two years ago today that Roger died. The vibrant young man whose ingenuity got him to the West Coast during the depression by carrying a bold red gas can that had GAS painted on one side, but a door cut out on the other so he could stuff a few belongings into it, waited patiently for death to overtake him. His greatest Christian testimony was the childlikeness of his spirit as he watched the Florida sunsets, knowing that soon one would finally be his last.

Maybe it's just because I was a doting sister—or maybe it's because I know that everybody loves things that contain human interest, so I'm going to recount here some of the hilarious things Roger did.

After he retired, he worked for the sanitation department before moving to Florida. An insistent, crotchety old lady called the department almost daily with first one complaint and then another. The whole department was nearly beside themselves when she called one day to say, "There is a squirrel making a nest in my eavestrough, and a woodpecker is ruining my favorite tree! Get someone out to help me right away."

Groaning, the department head said, "Send Roger. He'll quiet her down."

So, ol' Rog went his way, whistling his merry tune as those of us remember him doing so well. When he arrived, he plopped a ladder against the trough and quickly took care of the squirrel's nest. The little old lady eyed him coldly and chirped, "Well, sonny? Whatcha' goin' to do about that woodpecker?"

Rog put his arm around her and said, "Granny, got a little problem. You see I'm the squirrel-ly one, but the woodpecker man is on vacation, and won't be back for a couple of weeks, but I'll send him right out the minute he comes back. . . ."

Well, that was Roger. His Indiana snow shovel still stands propped up against the palm tree in front of his residence in Anna Maria, Florida. The mailbox that is towering in midair on a weaving ten-foot pole with AIR MAIL written on it still remains. And the good and tender memories still remain.

It had been Roger's decision to be cremated, so we never used the facilities of a funeral parlor. As we received long lines of sorrowing townsfolk, a policeman stepped up to my sister-in-law Hazel and remarked, "Mrs. Kendall, the law enforcement officers want to be of service. As is customary, we will provide an honor guard at the services." Hazel murmured her gratitude, and went on to other comforters in line.

The next day, the phone rang and it was for Hazel. She was stifling a much needed laugh. She said, "It was that policeman again . . . he said they'd run into a problem they'd never experienced before. It seems they don't know how to conjure up an honor guard—without a casket—or a body of some kind. . . ."

I roared! "Oh, if only Roger were here! He'd tell them to go look up 'rent-a-body' in the yellow pages!" And a tear trickled down my cheek as I looked again at the enlarged picture we had of him, looking wistfully into one of his beloved Florida sunsets.

Well, we did exactly as Roger would have wanted us to do. We entered immediately back into the flow of life, knowing that our times of farewell with one another would be at different times. This generation must pass away and the next will then begin to grow old, and likewise make ready for a departure into eternity. Yes, a departure into that other world—the one we were really created for. Our lives are truly but a vapor, a mist that appears for a while and then disappears, or like a flower that is soon scorched and withered away.

But that other life lies before us in all it's glory and with its hint of perfection. There, we shall finally come to have that Perfect Parent we've all been craving for—and those perfect relationships we long for down here on earth.

When I see all the pain and suffering that this old world has to offer it doesn't become a bit hard for me to lay up treasures in heaven, where neither moth nor rust corrupt.

Each day brings me comfortingly one day closer either to the coming of the Lord, or my coming home to be with Him. I truly have the longing for eternity deep in my heart. Lord, tell Roger it won't be long—we'll all be coming home soon, in God's good timing.

43

Last night I ran a nail through my foot clear up to my kneecap so today I'm still fussing and pouting around about it all. I've informed God that He'd better replace that angel that is supposed to be watching lest I dash my foot against a stone or at least give him a brush-up course on nail-piercing. But He reminded me that "all things work together for good" and because of my injury, I was able to con the kids into doing many of the things I usually do for them so I'd be able to make good use of this time to limp back into your hearts again, and also to wonder why I don't make them do some of those things all of the time, more often.

I was nursing the wound and just generally pampering my low threshold of pain when I decided to corrupt myself with some TV. I watched part of one of those insane situation comedies where pop is an absolute dolt, and mom has all the brains and realized that our children would come to accept this as an American way of life.

But the commercial was the killer! A slender gorgeous arm was seen pushing this miracle vacuum—with just the itsy-est bitsy-est pressure from the right index finger with such ease that it almost pushed itself. I thought, "Yeah, they told me that pierced ears wouldn't hurt, either."

First of all, if her duties have been so carefree, then why didn't her arm look like a huge ham hock? When her life has been made so simple, how does she burn up any calories?

Yet, I must confess, in spite of our many time-freeing devices, I'm genuinely exhausted when I creep into bed. I have this little callous on my index finger that comes from pushing the button on my washer, my dryer, my dishwasher, my light switches, my air conditioner, my toaster, the mixer, the TV, the garbage disposal, the garage door opener, the telephone, etc.

But still I have to face the fact that our lives *aren't* simple. We live at a pace in this country that drains us emotionally. And so much of our bustle is so unnecessary. When we stand before the Lord, is He going to hold us accountable for beautifully manicured lawns? For spotlessly clean homes? I think not. He will hold us accountable for those who stood before us with tears in their eyes. He will ask us how we responded to those who were hurting. He will know all about our motives that made us do what we've done—was it in love? Love for Him, for His people, with whom He identifies so closely?

And when we stand before Him, we will make the discovery that we so often failed to love our neighbor as ourself. The enemy comes in like a flood to give us a thousand reasons why our neighbor is not deserving of our love. He is divisive, but Jesus reconciles.

I really don't know what all this has to do with our slender lass with the pushy fingertip. But as I sit here with a flaming foot that hampers movement, I have time to take stock of my own heart. I have to readily admit that too often my motives are often based on self-love and self-aggrandizement. So what do I do? I do as Martin Luther did—he said, "I believe in grace, and the forgiveness of sins, and under this doth my weary heart creep." And so, under all this, doth my weary heart creep. But I'll leave my screaming foot out where the air can get to it. . . .

44

Wish I could "get my head together." I'm seeing foggily because of new trifocals, my pierced ears are screaming, my sinuses are clogged and I've a hunk of dental floss stuck between two inseparable teeth! If it were possible to laugh one's head off, I think I'd be inclined to try. I think with my heart most of the time, anyhow.

You know, I don't see why anyone would ever watch soap operas when they could just follow me around awhile and watch the real thing happen! In the midst of pampering my head, ears, sinuses and teeth, I got a phone call. It went something like this:

"Char? This is Liz. Do you have a few minutes? Man, do I need to talk. I've just made a discovery that has almost shattered me. Mom, as you know, hasn't been given too much time to live. Char, she pulled me down on the bed beside her and proceeded to tell me that my precious dad *wasn't even my father!* Good heavens! I'm a thirty-four-year-old woman and I'm shook to the core!"

"Liz, maybe it was just the delirious ravings of a very sick woman. . . ."

"No, Char—I checked with my two older sisters. They cried and went all to pieces, too, but they said they'd known

128

for years, because I was born when they were teenagers . . . honestly! Oh, Char, it only makes me love dad all the more . . . he's loved me as dearly as he has the others. I am so grateful to him! But he's obviously forgiven mom many years ago, so I'm not going to bring it up to him."

"That's good wisdom, Liz."

"But Char," she continued, "the other uncomfortable thing is, she told me *who my real father is* and I *know* him!"

I gulped. "Wow . . . makes me wonder if some things aren't better taken to the grave."

After the conversation, I thought about the whole situation. It is evident that sin needs to be confessed and forgiven, but to whom? To God, of course . . . but there is that basic need to confess to another person—what does the Word say? "Confess your faults one to another . . . that ye may be healed." And, "Bear ye one another's burdens." But what made this mother think that her burden of guilt would be relieved if the innocent daughter knew? She was certainly no part of the sin—merely a victim of circumstances.

By now I'd removed my earrings, freed the floss, blown my nose and decided to live with my glasses . . . but all the while, my heart is saying, "Hm-m-m." If God ever opens the door for such a thing as Christian soap operas, I've sure got a great store of ideas to draw from!

45

The books I've written have often been the means that God has used to drop some of the most delightful people into my life. I could almost write a book about these escapades alone, but then Chris and Dwight would let all the air out of my tires, and our precious dignified Sue, who has been such a blessing to us all, would whomp me one, and now, even as I relate the story of Mary—she will grin her quiet knowing smile and say, "Oh, wow. Never thought I'd wind up in a book!"

(I've always said that the next book I was going to write would probably be a telephone directory, because everyone seems to want their name in a book!)

Mary just came into my life last week. She called and said, "I just read your book. May I come and visit you sometime?" I set a time, and as I sat there, enjoying her so very much, I couldn't help but think of how quietly God is going about His business of building His church.

Her three children were playing nicely close by as Mary related her story. Her husband had left her two and a half years ago. She'd only moved into our area two months prior to the time we were sharing. Someone had handed her about five books to read, and one of them was my first book. As she read, she was aware that I lived somewhere where the winters were severe . . . then she saw that I called myself a "Hoosier." As she finished the last chapter, she saw an open telephone book before her, almost like a vision, she remarked. She felt that was God's way of prompting her to look in the directory, and she said she almost fainted when she saw my name and realized that we were in the same community.

Mary fascinated me. Life had dealt her some very tough blows, but her serenity and yieldedness to Christ were so beautiful to see.

Mary is caring for her brother who is a paraplegic. Quietly, she went on to tell me that her mother was not caring for him because she and another brother had been killed in the Palm Sunday tornado that had struck our area, and did I recall this tornado?

I was nearly taken aback when I realized that here was another tragedy this little thing had withstood, when all the memories of the Palm Sunday came flooding back to me . . . how vividly I recalled my fear because my little daughter was at her friend's house and it was hours before we knew if she was even alive . . . the somber blackness that surrounded us . . . the employee who made his way to our back door, groping in the darkness, to weep out his sorrow. He'd found his little son dead in the debris that had once been his home. He didn't know if his wife and daughter were dead or alive. Yes, I very painfully remembered the Palm Sunday tornado.

Mary went on with her conversation. "I've been praying about a place to fellowship . . . could you tell me about yours?" Yes, Mary. In fact, I want to tell everyone. I'd like to tell the entire world about the glorious thing God is doing in our area. Quietly, softly, here a little and there a little, He is bringing those who are hurting to the place where we meet as His church. We seem to be a people who are being prepared as a congregation to . . . well, just let me tell you about it.

46

Hm-m-m. Now that I've got you curious about the fellowship, how do I begin? I'm afraid you've already started to yawn, or are reaching for your bookmark . . . or considering a nap . . . or thinking, "If you've seen one fellowship, you've seen 'em all."

I realize, too, that church history can be a drag. Well, life can be a drag, too, if you don't keep it ignited with the fire of the Holy Spirit, so I'll be praying that He will breathe a bit of spirit and life into all this so you won't be overcome with ennui. In fact, why don't you just curl up on my lap while I tell you about us? That way, if you should fall asleep, I'll still be holding you close.

First, a bit of drowsy background music. (If Gene were here, he'd be dramatically sawing away at an imaginary violin, while sighing, as I made my way into, "I was raised . . ." but fortunately he is diligently providing for his family . . . plus slaving "by the sweat of his brow" to pay off this ridiculously high-priced typewriter he bought me in a moment of weakness.)

(Ahem-m-m.) I was raised in a non-Christian home with a father who could only face life when he was tipsy, but my love for him is too strong to ever call him a drunk, and he didn't have enough sophistication to bear the title of "alcoholic." I guess maybe "thick-tongued, irresistible and irresponsible" would best describe him. Mom dabbled in what she called "spiritualism" but what I realize now should more appropriately have been called "spiritism." I was always repelled by this, and as I look back, I see that I was also greatly protected from it by a loving God who has every one of my days recorded in His book, and knows the end of my life, as well as all other parts.

Even as a child, I had strong stirrings in my heart godward, and I seemed to know instinctively that I should have nothing to do with mom's beliefs.

After Gene and I had been married for about five years these stirrings became so intense, I could no longer strive against that very thing I needed the most—reconciliation with my creator through His Son, Jesus Christ. We became part of an institutional church that was full of solid Bible teaching. As I look back now, I feel we were thrust into "responsibility" too soon. Too much emphasis on "doing" without experiencing the necessary growing pains of "becoming."

I made the mistake of drawing all my strength from the "fellowship of the saints" and the pastor, as if they could do no wrong. I was so young, so impetuous, with no idea of what a fine line there was between being vivacious . . . and being flirtatious. I did the very thing that I now move heaven and earth to avoid in the lives of young women I'm dealing with . . . I allowed the pastor to become my husband's rival. You see I had to learn experientially that my heart was wicked and deceitful and very capable of inordinate affections . . . affections that are "out of bounds."

But God has such a blessed way of making something wonderful out of the messes we get ourselves into. When I went to my precious husband and confessed that I had permitted my heart to become weaned away from him, he took me in his arms and confessed that he'd almost allowed something valuable to slip away from him by not noticing, or caring. (The learning experience was so meaningful, we vowed to one another that if we found this ever happening, we'd immediately admit the seeming attraction, as we discovered that the enemy will withdraw when his tactics are exposed to the light of confession.)

But I remember a prophetic utterance I made at that time. I said, "Gene, I really blew a relationship that God had trusted me with . . . but somewhere, down through the years, God is going to give me back that privilege . . . I know that He will someday allow me a close relationship with a pastor. A relationship that is pure, effective, and ordained of Him."

This crisis caused me to draw my strength from Christ and Christ alone. As I drew closer to Him, I gradually became aware of how very legalistic and authoritative this denomination was. God was broadening my horizons, and I had to follow Him, no matter what people said or thought.

I then received the baptism of the Holy Spirit and found myself right in the middle of the charismatic movement and all of its problems. I say that lovingly, because no move of God is without its problems. A particular adversary sees to that!

But the fellowship we attended was in another town. The distance, plus horrendous winters, plus the growing belief that God wants you involved with those in your own local area made us aware that we should find a place closer to home. We found nothing with a charismatic flavor to it, so back to the institutional church to learn more valuable lessons. In the meantime, a process of stagnation was beginning to penetrate. Finally, one day, in desperation I cried out to God. "Father, I can't believe that you love others more than you do us . . . there *has* to be a place for us . . . please lead us to it."

And He did! Like I started to say a chapter or so ago . . . lemme tell you about our fellowship. . . .

47

Pictorially speaking, I usually think of our fellowship as the "hand" of the body of Christ. Contentedly speaking, I'm happy to say that it is not a tight fist of condemnation nor are the fingernails bit to the quick because of legalism. The oil of gladness flows freely over it from the top of the pastor's head to the hem of his garments, and then throughout the entire congregation, so it doesn't become dry . . . or flaky.

It reminds me of Christ's hand, because so many nails are being driven through it with a constancy that smacks of urgency, and makes me wonder . . . is He coming soon? The hammer blows sound as though they are getting closer together throughout the fellowship, and the groans of His people are crying for relief, yet bearing fruit. And every time we find some fruit coming to maturity, and place it in that hand, that hand begins to exert pressure on us and we become poured out wine before we know what's happened!

Now, you'll feel a bit silly, as though we are playing "this little piggy went to market" but enter into my word picture with childlikeness and examine that hand with me. Our pastor is here, on the index finger. His name is Luther Hasz, but known to us affectionately as Lu. I don't mean to imply, by comparing him with the index finger, that he ever points accusingly at us . . . although he'd probably be the first to admit that he fights the temptation to do so, occasionally. No, he points us to the cross, and to that precious Christ who hung upon it. Then he points us heavenward and to that same Christ who now sits at the right hand of the Father, and gently Lu says, "If you want to live in the heavenlies with this same Jesus, you must take that cross for your own, and carry it daily, doggedly, without flinching, without a backward glance, without grumbling, without murmuring." But he doesn't leave us there, alone. He then becomes like Simon of Cyrene who got under the load of the cross with Jesus, and he helps us bear it by interceding and caring for us with the pastor's heart that God has given him, for Christ's sake, and for ours.

Beside the index finger are the strengthening "support" fingers. These are the elders, the deacons, the men of the congregation who trust the Christ in Luther, and who have eternity in their hearts, flowing in and with God, under Lu's leadership.

The little finger, so dainty and small, sometimes seeming a bit useless, yet adding so much grace and charm to the whole hand, reminds us of the children in our fellowship. Fragile, easily hurt, getting in where they shouldn't, but always a part of us, bringing beauty and balance . . . and hope to us . . . hope for the future.

And ladies, like it or not, *we* are the thumb! Most of us are broader than we'd like to be, and so often "shorter" when it comes to the good solid logic available to our men. And it runs in my mind that the thumb almost always bears more of the hammer blows . . . because (ahem) it's usually in the way. But it's the only part of the hand that can be tucked so safely under the other three fingers beside it. The authority that God has given our men is our protection, no matter how much we chafe against it.

Have you ever thought of what it would be like to go through life without a thumb? Try turning pages, picking up lint, opening any number of things without that funny-looking, exasperating thumb. That thumb is a source of great comfort to many babies. And that thumb is almost always working in conjunction with the index finger. I know there are times when that index finger wishes he never had a thumb to contend with! Yet, he knows he'd be hampered without it . . . and is much blessed because of it.

There have been times when the whole hand has been aflame with pain because of a cut, a bruise, a broken bone somewhere on a finger, but the body of Christ is like our own body. It has the potential of bringing healing from within itself. At the first indication of injury, the antibodies (prayers) are discharged. The intercessors flood the area with tears and supplications, becoming "white cells" oozing with care and concern to meet the situation. The healing process begins and the hand becomes "whole" again.

Well, you are right. Fellowships are very much alike. Especially when they are controlled by the Holy Spirit. But to me, our little band is very special. Oh, some of us aren't really pretty. And some are very lovely to look at. Some of us walk funny. Some of us swallow funny. Some of us laugh funny, and some of us *are* funny. But we are being cemented together with a bond of love with what you might call —"Epox-agape" glue. The "can't budge, won't crack, sealed-in-earnest" kind of love. But just let us know if you ever need a helping "hand." We'll be there!

48

We were homeward bound and passing through the southern part of Indiana when a quaint sign caught my eye. It read "COVERED BRIDGE" with an arrow pointing westward, ho.

"Oh, Gene! It can't be too far away—it would be great if the kids could see a bit of Hoosier history close-up . . . please?" I wheedled.

Gene started muttering and expostulating about "Humph! Spend most of my life behind a wheel, and she wants to take a detour . . ." but he grinned and turned according to the arrow, in spite of his longing to be home before dark. We drove . . . and drove . . . through cow paddies, back roads, low branches and chuckholes, to finally arrive at our destination.

I got out of the car so I could caress the worn boards that reeked with historical significance while framing feminine "oo's" and "ah-h-h's" as I approached the phenomenon. But the closer I got, the more I expressed tongue in cheek "oh-oh's" as I discovered the bridge was covered, all right—with obscenities. I managed to continually lurch ahead of the children by about ten paces, flailing myself against the walls at awkward intervals while my children (who were small at the time) stomped through the relic making appreciative comments like, "Why'd we drive so far out of our way to look at this dumb thing? I could build a better one with Lincoln logs," and "Mom, what does this word mean?" as I flung myself against the opposite wall with a Mary Poppins flair.

Gene is nearly hysterical and making little snide comments like, "What shall we do for an encore—take them to a porno movie?" and "Hm-m-m. They did a good job. They didn't misspell a thing."

We all made our way back to the car, the kids resuming a previous argument as to who, after all, should get to sit in the front seat and mom really should ride in the trunk for making dad go all this way to see that crummy old bridge. I was grateful that within ten minutes they forgot the bridge, their need for a potty and their craving for the nearest McDonald's, and were cozily asleep. Gene picked up all of his orderly, businessman thoughts he'd been engrossed in previously, and I was lost in a muddled reverie of thinking how funny it is that things always look so much more romantic on a movie screen than when it is "for real." I never once saw an obscenity in a travelogue—or muddy water, pop cans and candy wrappers and mud.

And then, being deeply philosophical the way I am, I couldn't help thinking, "Wow, that's really how life is. Things look so great from a distance, but up close they often have a taint, a burden that clings to them. You give birth to a precious and beautiful baby—it comes complete with icky-poo diapers and temper tantrums. You fall in love with someone, then discover their imperfections. You acquire a home—it has to be scrubbed constantly. Get a swimming pool, then find out about all the upkeep. (People used to ask us, as they were sunning themselves around our pool, "When do you know to clean the pool?" and I'd reply,

140

"When the guests come up draped in seaweed, that's when.")

Every blessing carries its own particular burden with it. But if that is so, isn't it only reasonable to think that then, perhaps, every burden has a hidden blessing within someplace? I think the two always walk hand in hand and I think God would even agree with me, or else why would He tell us to praise Him in all things? Could it just be that He is working out His purposes for our lives in the midst of trials as well as in prosperity? What lesson can come from the covered bridge?

Hm-m-m. Well, I can share with the kids that yes, there are things in life that are very beautiful, but sin has marred and placed its mark on everything. The continual reminder that we are fallen creatures living in the midst of those who want to pull down, destroy and deface needn't discourage us, but only make us realize our need of a Savior, who will take us from all this and bring us into a glorious existence someday free from the taint of sin. And with a good moral like that tucked away in my heart to throw at them when they woke up, I fell asleep myself. (I only hope you didn't!)

49

This morning was really a bad scene with one of my sons.
For his sake, I'll let him remain anonymous. He dawdled,
fussed, missed his bus, and was generally reeking with
teenage rebellion. Was I the understanding tender mother
God meant for me to be? About as far from that as thunder is
from the still small voice of God.

The whole thing had to do with one load of undone
laundry, two arms that were growing more rapidly than I
realized, and three little words that took too long in coming
out. I'm going to relate the complete sordid fiasco to you, with
fear and trembling, as I know that someday my husband and
my pastor will probably read this. (They may both decide to
punch my lights out! Simultaneously!)

Scenario begins: Yawning, harassed, fighting-flu-bug
mother realizes that alarm was set for wrong time. Makes way
gropingly to inner recesses of second story where various
bodies are draped, snoring, gulping, and snitziling. (That is no
error. I just can't think of another word that fits that special
sound that goes with the early morning can't-face-the-day
syndrome.)

Mother says, fussily: "We're late"—(cracks
fanny—child's, I mean). "Get a hustle on, and come on

down and eat."

Sleeper: "Uh-hum-m. Be right down-z-z-z-z ... ick, glump—right away-z-z-z-."

Mother: With firmer crack on snuggled-in fanny, "Hey! I *mean* it! Right now! Up and at 'em."

Mother makes way to kitchen, fumbles around getting breakfast while endeavoring to get cobwebs out of numb brain. With a pang, realizes that one particular body hasn't revived enough to sidle into niche at breakfast counter.

Mother yells: "What *IS* the hold-up? What are you *DOING!*"

From nether regions upstairs: "Ma, I can't find a shirt that fits—can't find one that will go with these pants—where *is* everything?"

Mother in self-defense: "That's ridiculous! All the wash is done"—*oops! the load with shirts—I'd meant to do that—hum-m-m.* "You've plenty of shirts up there!" (Mother makes dramatic strides up stairs with martyr-like sighs escaping from between clenched teeth.) "See? You've a *closet* full!"

Downcast teenager: "Ma, look—" as he tries shirts on, exposing huge wrists, bulging biceps that can't be covered—growth too soon, too rapid for mother to take in.

Mother: "It can't be—I—well, that's no excuse. Put on a different pair of pants—you've shirts that will go with blue jeans—you can wear your cords another day." Mother retreats in a huff, hearing son state, "I'm just a rotten kid, I guess."

(Author's note: Martyred mother not yet familiar enough with active listening to jump on the bandwagon. Correction: Mother aware of active listening and need for it, but too limp to know how to react. Correction: Too *stubborn* to react properly; finds that active screaming more suited to mood. . . .)

Dejected and forlorn child enters: Silence reigns.

Mother responds, hostility melting, somewhat: "You'd better eat. You are late already. A few more minutes won't make that much difference."

Morose child: "I'm not hungry."

Repentant mother: "Honey, why do we do this to one another? I really do love you!" (First entrance, front and center, of three necessary and vital words . . . three more necessary words yet to come.)

Child, with touch of interest: "I don't know, ma—maybe I *could* eat a bite. . ." as he proceeds to devour breakfast.

Mother, who is now dying a thousand inward deaths begins to purr: "Tell you what. I'll do my part if you'll do yours." (Weak response, but mothers aren't perfect, y' know.)

Child answers, while smearing peanut butter off of finger on adjoining kitchen stool. "Whatdya' mean?"

Mother, cringing inwardly while gently handing him a napkin and gesturing toward neighboring kitchen stool. "I'll go through the drawers, clear out everything that is too small, and we'll go buy some new clothes, and you start putting your things out at night, so we don't have this hassle in the mornings." (Mother makes negative mental note: How many times in the past thirty years has such a suggestion worked? Only twice—with both daughters. Not only did they lay their clothes out—they started at four o'clock in the afternoon, put five combinations together, tried them all on, left discarded ones in a heap, and resorted to a ten-thirty phone call—"Stacy? Do you have something I can borrow to wear tomorrow? Oh good—my red blouse? With the fake patches? You want that? Okay—I'll trade with you as soon as we get to school. . . .")

144

Mother deposits erring child at school. Child brightens as he sees peer group—probably can't wait to tell them what a rotten mother he has.

Mother returns home. Calls school to explain why child is tardy. Pleasant voice says, "No need to explain . . . your son told us he missed the bus."

Mother weeps quietly before the Lord. "Father, forgive me. I've blown it again. My son could have blamed me for not getting the shirts done, for not setting the alarm properly, for being such a grouch. But instead, he just said he missed the bus. Lord, I told him I loved him—but I didn't mention those other three necessary words—'please forgive me.' I know that 'all things work together for good' so would you please allow something beautiful to come out of this little charade you witnessed today? My trust is in you, Lord. Bridge the gap between what happened, and what should have happened here this morning . . . between what was said, and what should have been said. Speak a special peace to his heart right now, Father. I know that you've forgiven me. Now let me talk it out with him tonight. Thank you, Lord. Amen."

End of scenario? Hardly. For the present moments have a way of making their way into the future, leaving the memories of the past to hurt, crush, irritate, bless or whatever, depending on whether or not you've brought them before the Lord to be dealt with. For our sins *have* been forgiven. Our hurts *have* been healed. Our irritations *have* been quieted—but only in the Lord.

50

I came across this letter in my files on the very day that I had had the uncomfortable to-do with my son. After reading it again, I couldn't wait for him to come home from school so I could make more definite amends. The letter, taken from *To Kiss the Joy* by Robert A. Raines, was written by an anonymous youthful runaway, and I share it with you:

Dear Folks:
Thank you for everything, but I am going to Chicago and try and start some kind of new life. You asked me why I did those things and why I gave you so much trouble, and the answer is easy for me to give you, but, I am wondering if you will understand.
Remember when I was about six or seven and I used to want you to just listen to me? I remember all the nice things you gave me for Christmas and my birthday, and I was really happy with the things—for about a week—at the time I got the things, but the rest of the time during the year I really didn't want presents. I just wanted all the time for you to listen to me like I was somebody who felt things too, because I remember even when I was young I felt things. But you said you were busy.

Mom, you are a wonderful cook, and you had everything so clean and you were tired so much from doing all those things that made you busy; but, you know something, mom? I would have liked crackers and peanut butter just as well if you had only sat down with me awhile during the day and said to me, "Tell me all about it so I can maybe help you understand!"

And when Donna came I couldn't understand why everyone made so much fuss because I didn't think it was my fault that her hair is curly and her skin so white and she doesn't have to wear glasses with such thick lenses. Her grades were better too, weren't they? If Donna ever has children, I hope you will tell her to just pay some attention to the one who doesn't smile very much because that one will really be crying inside. And when she's about to bake six dozen cookies, to make sure first that the kids don't want to tell her about a dream or a hope or something, because thoughts are important, too, to small kids even though they don't have so many words to use when they tell about what they have inside them.

I think that all the kids who are doing so many things that grown-ups are tearing out their hair worrying about are really looking for somebody that will have time to listen a few minutes and who really and truly will treat them as they would a grown-up who might be useful to them. You know—polite to them. If you had ever said to me: "Pardon me" when you interrupted me, I'd have dropped dead! If anybody asks you where I am, tell them I've gone looking for somebody with time because I've got a lot of things I want to talk about.

Love to all,
Your Son.

51

Getting to the bottom of the ironing basket is, for most people, a milestone, a happening. For me, it is damaging, for alas! I see that all the styles have changed! And so, to keep my mind off my strong inclinations toward procrastination, I'm going to really make your day by zapping you with a story that has a moral to it. Might just be really refreshing, seeing as how we live in such a demoralized society.

We have a friend who is a pastor in another city. One of his flock was continually giving the parish trouble as he was always saying that he would do something, or buy someone something, with nary an intention of carrying the promise out. One day, our friend the pastor walked up to him and said, "Hi, Joe . . . say, that's a snazzy shirt. Where'd you get it?"—momentarily forgetting the fellow's weakness.

"Oh, this?" responded Joe. "You really like it? Hey, I'll buy you one. Sure thing, I will." He beamed. With this, our quick-witted friend parried with, "Fine, Joe. Meet me tomorrow, as soon as you get off work. I'll just let you buy me one, and just to be sure you get the right size, I'll even go with you. Wow, I really like it . . . sure hope they have one left . . . see ya' . . . after work tomorrow . . . 'bye." And the pastor left a perplexed Joe standing there.

Later that night, our friend the pastor called Joe's wife. He said, "Sue, I'm going to reimburse you for the cost of the shirt Joe's going to buy me. I know you kids are strapped, but I feel like Joe needs to know the 'cost' of discipleship. I don't think God wants us to go around saying we'll do things we have no intention of carrying out. Joe needs to find out how expensive idle words can be. Will you be my accomplice in this? If it seems a bit deceptive, God will hold me responsible, not you."

Sue was elated. "It'll be an object lesson he'll never forget," she laughed.

Well, Joe bought him the shirt, and Joe learned to "put his money where his mouth was." But what about the rest of us? Have you ever had a brother or sister in Christ tell you, "Let me know when I can be of any help," and then, when you let them know that you are in a pinch, you make the discovery that those little words are just hollow, trite, and often said only because it is the right thing to say? But lessons like this cause you to watch what comes out of your own mouth.

I'm very careful about telling others I'll baby-sit if I don't feel that's what I want to do. However, emergencies do happen, and I will pinch-hit . . . well, I really never pinch or hit when baby-sitting, but you know what I mean.

But I'm learning that speaking the truth in love is a matter of speaking what you really feel, but in *His* love, so that the other person is not devastated. It's called "risky loving." But we do need to examine our hearts, rinse out our motives and put feet to our intentions. We need to remember that too often "I can't" means, more realistically, "I don't want to." Why don't we just be honest? It's a good policy, y'know.

52

Today I received another "grammy award." I was getting lunch, and two toddlers grabbed me, an arm around each leg, and looked up at me from that far distance that to them must make me appear like the jolly green giant. One grinned and hugged me tighter, and the other was just old enough to say, "I wuv you, grammy." Of course my senile ol' heart melted into a lump of sugar and I somehow managed to scoop them both into my arms, knocking over a glass of juice, just like in the good ol' days. They smelled so good, and felt so soft. But then again, they said I did too. Which is vastly encouraging. Unless soft was the extent of their vocabulary which would have come out "fat" at a later date? Hm-m-m.

And I realized, that someday one of them would come up to me and say, "Tell me about when you were little." And I would become a bit dreamy-eyed and try to describe for them what it was like to hear the horse-drawn milk wagons go along Grandma Yarnell's brick street in front of her house in Grand Rapids . . . and I'd try to help them hear the sound of the trains when they were still a bit mournful and full of sadness instead of the ulcer-shattering diesels they'll remember. I'd try to imitate the pleasant clickety-click of the old hand mowers that soothed—as long as you weren't the one pushing the impossible monstrosity. And I'd tell them about the corner grocers!

(When we were in England, the corner grocers were such a nostalgic delight to me. It was not unusual to buy a loaf of unwrapped bread, toss it into your personal shopping bag, then lean across the counter and chat, or just listen to neighbors sharing, or bragging about their children. But here in America, the cold sterility of the supermarket leaves me feeling a bit lonely in our advanced society.)

While on a speaking engagement once, I did run across a small grocer. I was sorry I didn't have the time to soak up some of his atmosphere, and after I got to the car, I realized I'd probably paid dearly for the "atmosphere" I *had* soaked up as I figured up how little my purchase would have cost in a supermarket. But an interesting thing happened, as I asked God's forgiveness for being a poor steward of His money. Quietly, He said, "You haven't been. The owner is elderly, and would have a difficult time getting employment anywhere else. He has to charge a higher price, because of overhead and small clientele. I never intended that my money should be pinched and held back from others." And I then remembered a principle I'd seen in Leviticus. Simply stated, the principle is that of leaving some for others. At the next long train—an uninteresting, nasal sounding diesel freight train—I looked it up. "And thou shalt not glean thy vineyard, neither shalt thou gather every grape of thy vineyard; thou shalt leave them for the poor and stranger: I am the Lord your God" (Lev. 19:10).

Hm-m-m. Well, I'm not sure what all this has to do with anything else I've included in this chapter, but you can get away with little inconsistencies when you're not a professional writer or Nobel prize seeker. "Grammy" awards will do nicely, thank you.

53

I'm feeling a bit moody right now, but it isn't an unpleasant moodiness. Nor is it a melancholy. It's a touch of disappointment mingled with unfulfilled expectations. Somewhere within me, "deep is calling unto deep," and no other being has responded. On two occasions today, I'd expected to have truly stimulating conversation, but for God's own reasons, the conversation never moved beyond the superficial humdrum. Everything within me was poised for vibrant rapport, perhaps even an exchange of wit, but now I'm allowing the desire to be at least thumbtacked to the cross, or blown away like dandelion-down. For it really isn't that important. Pleasing others should be satisfying enough, shouldn't it? And other people *did* seem to enjoy the conversation.

I suppose I made my first mistake by thinking that others were seeking the same thing I was. The second mistake was placing my expectations any place but in God. Do you ever do that? Thinking that the satisfaction will come from a particular getting-together of people who are special to you . . . or placing too much eager anticipation into a looked-for event? I thought I'd outgrown this immaturity, somewhat, but after today, I'm not so sure.

I know why God allows this to happen. It keeps us poor in spirit. I realize that the longing I feel in my heart right now can only be filled by Him, but He needs to remind me of this so that I will not look to man for the satisfaction that only He can give. The longing acts as a continual reminder.

Gene says that we also need to be very careful, as it is possible to become spiritually selfish. *I'm* happier if we are talking about the Lord, something He's been up to, or searching the Word. But not all people are longing for this, yet. *I'm* happier if the Spirit of God is hovering over our conversation, flooding it with His special anointing . . . but not all know how to handle this.

So, I must learn that real Christian maturity comes when we are willing to talk about whatever interests others . . . or real maturity comes when we are willing to say little, yet still caring . . . or when we are willing for others to carry the mainstream of the conversation. It has something to do with "not sitting in the highest place" but with a quiet willingness to be called up to a "higher" place. *Maybe.*

But tomorrow is a fresh beginning. I will apply the lessons learned today, and see that my "expectations" come from Him. And, when I'm least looking for it—that stimulating conversation will spring up in my life! *Maybe* . . .

54

Jamie is growing up. So much so, that he wants to be called Jim. "But, mom," he grins, "you can always call me Jamie, I guess. Just don't ever hug and kiss me and junk like that in front of my friends, mom."

How quickly those years fly by. It seems like only yesterday when I was blustering before the Lord, "Father, you've got to be kidding! Another baby? Where will we put it? How will I cope? Don't you know I've got more than I can handle right now? Are you sure you've got the right address? I mean, Lord . . . I've got five now!" And I made a big thing about reminding God that I'd just starved myself down into a size eleven, and thinking it couldn't be possible, especially since I'd been having so much abdominal pain—better check with the doctor . . . that peppy, won't-stay-put doctor of mine who'd been out shooting the rapids some place in Colorado when I tried to get in for an appointment just a few weeks ago.

I went to her, as soon as she was back in town. She examined me, plucked a gray hair out of my head, grinned and said, "You may have a few more of these before it's over. . . ."

"Babies?" I spluttered. "Hey, I've done my stint at replenishing. . . ."

"No, silly—I mean gray hairs. Yes, you are going to have a baby. But I'm also scheduling you for surgery at the very earliest date after the baby arrives . . . can't do it until the child is four months old. Char, it's interesting—didn't you tell me that you tried to make an appointment a few weeks ago? If I'd been here, I'd have scheduled you for surgery immediately. Well, it looks like God has other plans for you. . . ."

"Yeah . . . how 'bout that," I responded a bit weakly. Well, God, being God the way He is, changed my attitude before Jamie arrived. Many times I would think about the "mystery" concerning his conception and birth. Did God have something special for this child? I've always thought so.

Jamie's life has been full of interesting "things." For instance, my sister Lauraine got all excited because Jamie, at age four, begged me to buy him some kind of "doctor book" that would tell him all about the heart, and muscles, and what makes the blood move in our bodies. I found a simplified "human body" book, and could hardly believe it when it became his favorite bedtime fare! And he wouldn't be put down for a nap until we'd read a few pages and talked about the pictures. Naturally, she and I thought we'd come up with some kind of a genius. It was kind of a jolt to find out that when he did enter school, he had little interest for learning at all. Music, from the time he could tap out a beat on his highchair with first two Q-tips, and later, two unsharpened pencils, consumed his entire waking moments.

His pictorial world of nerve ends, scabs, and muscle layers fell away to drums, beats, even to the point of his thinking how groovy the washing machine was because it "had a real beat to it."

Obviously, I had a problem on my hands. The school system in our area had this thing about learning, and didn't get too excited about natural ability, and things like that.

In fact, I soon discovered that Jamie and I had a *real* struggle on our hands. *His* cross was following in the footsteps of Mark and Laurie who'd excelled tremendously, scholastically. Mine was in realizing that I'd failed him miserably by not making him a more responsible person. He'd developed poor habits, and I just kept thinking, "Some day, he'll change." Teachers weren't so sure. I remember well the agonizing hour I'd spent in the principal's office with the school counselor. We all agreed that Jamie needed some kind of motivation, so that he would somehow feel prompted to do his work, without nagging from my end.

With great assurance, I said, "It will happen, someday."

Quietly, the principal remarked, "But what if it doesn't? What then?"

I stood there in stunned silence. I felt God's love surging through every fiber of my being. I turned slowly from the door and faced him. I felt a familiar trembling within me as I said, "Sir, I make my requests to a miracle-working God. I settle for nothing less *than* a miracle-working God. In His own timing, it will happen, and it will be soon enough. I refuse to believe anything other than this." And with that, I walked out . . . but not too late to hear the counselor say, in an awestruck way, "That's beautiful. . . ."

Yes, I knew that Jamie needed motivation. He had to find some rhyme or reason as to why music couldn't reign supreme, and why schooling was important. Now that he's entered junior high, some of this is coming together. But I think last night . . . he got it even more "together."

His school sponsored a "rock concert." I wasn't too excited—but knowing how much music means to Jamie, I paid for what I felt was a rather expensive ticket for the affair. He didn't come home until late—I was rather upset. Didn't know where he was, and why he hadn't called for a ride home.

Finally, the phone rang. "Mom, come and get me and I'll tell you why I'm late—don't be mad, mom—please."

When I picked him up, he hopped into the car and stammered, "Mom, I'm late because—well, these guys were Christians, mom, and they talked with me—in fact, they prayed with me . . . mom, I've given my heart and life back to Christ—you know I haven't been too interested lately, but mom—these guys—they really care about God and stuff like that—and they even said that I could play their drums—mom, when they heard me, they want me to audition so that I can travel with them after I graduate."

Quite frankly, I wanted to hop out of the car and do a pirouette right there in the middle of the traffic, but knew I had to keep my cool, so I quietly said, "What was the group called?"

"Young American Showcase, Inc. Mom, do you know what it would mean to me, to be able to use my music, and not be worried about getting into situations where everyone is a dope-head? Where drinking wouldn't be a part of the scene? And Ma, I could do it, and still help kids, and Jesus, too—ma, I'm so excited."

But I knew it was a quiet, thoughtful excitement. I could feel it. And I was so grateful to one Vinny Greco, for caring about my son's relationship to Christ.

Granted, the enemy got in his licks—with "he only did it to be accepted . . . it'll wear off . . . it's a cop-out."

Well, time will tell . . . but I do remember often the facts about his birth—how had the doctor been in, when I made that first phone call, there would be no Jamie now—except God had a plan for him, and for us, as part of Jamie's life. He's only a little over thirteen, right now. Yes, time will tell. And more than likely, so will I, if you care to listen. . . .

55

God's timing is *so* exciting. In *Thanks Lord, I Needed That!* I told you the story of a truly courageous woman by the name of "Frostie." She was fighting a battle with cancer, and in the book I related the instance of our meeting, and of what a blessing she'd been to me.

What I didn't incorporate into her story, simply because it didn't have much bearing at the time, was Frostie's insistence that I "simply must meet her niece," Sister Nora Frost who happened to be a Lutheran sister, an official deaconess of the Lutheran Church.

I really did have a desire to meet her niece, but I remember saying that, in God's time, it would probably happen. This was about three years ago.

Then, *my* niece started going with a fine young man who had been previously "messed up" but had been tremendously helped by "Sister Nora." Somehow, that rang a bell with me, but I wasn't yet aware of her last name.

Down through the months, I heard Sister Nora's name mentioned many times—so many times, that I found myself not only praying for her, but praying that God would make His arrangements so that we would meet soon. Now that I was a Lutheran, I had a special interest in knowing a "Sister" up close—so I could write about her!

Last month, I attended the county prayer and praise meeting. Maybe it was the gleam in her eye—maybe it was her quiet smile—but realistically, I think it was the obvious deaconess attire she was wearing, but I knew immediately, that this had to be the Sister Nora Frost that God had planned for me to meet at this given time.

Why, you are asking, do I take the time to relate all this? Because I've discovered that Sister Nora is a walking miracle, and I think you need to know that. (So there!)

You see, after the meeting, we all decided to have a cup of coffee at a local restaurant. Sister Nora sat beside me and I was elated to have the chance to get better acquainted with her, and to see if my memory wasn't playing tricks on me—that this *was* the niece Frostie had been telling me about.

"Yes," Sister Nora replied. "If it hadn't been for my aunt's courage, I'd never been able to take what I've taken since January."

My anointed nosiness was about to run again, when someone else ran away with the conversation in another direction, so I just tucked that away for future nosey reference.

At a later point in the somewhat disjointed but rollicking discourse, another person asked Nora a bit more about her Aunt Frostie. Nora answered their query, then turned to me, touched my arm lightly, and softly said, "Char, I only hope that others will be helped by my story when my time comes." Inwardly, I was asking, *Lord, what is she trying to tell me?* But again, the conversation lurched into another vein.

But her words came back to me that night just before I dropped off to sleep . . . and twice during the night, as I turned over . . . *when my time comes . . . when my time comes.*

Sister Nora and I had lunch together the next week. She commented about how cold she was "but then" she went on "that's not unusual when you don't have any blood."

I faced her. "Sister, somehow something keeps bugging me . . . those remarks you've made about your aunt . . . what are you trying to keep from telling us?"

We were in the ladies' room, and she was quietly brushing her hair. For a long moment, she didn't say anything. Finally, she said, "I do have a blood problem. I had surgery in January, but it didn't correct the situation . . . but as long as I stay transfused, I do quite well."

I've never been one for quiet tact. "Sister, what *is* the problem?"

She looked thoughtful. "My bone marrow does not produce enough red blood cells."

The knot in my stomach absorbed my unspoken reaction— *leukemia!* Verbally, I just said, "Oh—I see" as I remembered my recent experience with my brother Roger.

"But I have an unusual situation," she continued, "in fact, I have to be very careful, because I never feel pain. Even with my surgery, I never felt one bit of pain, and this is both a blessing and a burden, as I can't tell when I have a problem. Right now, my hemoglobin is only five and accordingly, I should be sick in bed. But my desire is just to keep working—my work is my life. I guess that's why I'm reluctant to call the disease by its right name. Word gets around, and then people start setting limitations and 'hovering.' I don't want that to happen."

"But sister, you are truly a walking miracle . . . may I write your story now?"

Her twenty-eight-year-old youthfulness made her radiant.

She laughed. "Don't you think you should wait until I die?"

I grinned. "Sister, when God comes to call you out of that body, I can see it now—you will look at Him, pat His hand and say, 'I know you mean well, but sir—I have all these hurting people in my parish, and you'll just have to wait a spell . . . you don't mind now, do you?' If I wait until He takes you home to be with Him, I may be too senile to write it. . . ."

It was such a thrill, to be able to talk so lightly, almost frivolously about the unknown future. Yet, God is permitting her to function normally, under sick bed statistics! No, not normally—but miraculously! I think He intends to leave our Sister Nora with us for some time.

When I shared with her that our pastor was always teasing me to "please bring in some healthy ones—just a few, Char, instead of all these sick ones . . ." she giggled and said, "When I come to visit, I'll let you come ahead of me—holding a bag of plasma, or toting an IV—" And we laughed, because in Christ, it is permissible to enter into His joy, even with an uncertain future staring you in the face. Realistically, we talked about not knowing what each day held, for anyone. No one knows what the future holds. But the two of us were "wrapped up in the bundle of life" for those few moments, and we were secure in knowing who holds our futures. That was enough.

56

I really didn't want to go to the coffee. Work was piling up at home and mice were beginning to nest in the undone laundry. I'd even tacked an "eat at your own risk" sign on the refrigerator shelf that housed the leftovers (on the ptomaine antidote slip I keep nearby).

But love and fellowship and huggin' and kissin' always have held a greater allurement than duty, so I powdered my nose, put a bubonic plague sign on the door so no one would enter, and sailed off to the coffee.

But as I drove, I wondered . . . what would I find? How would the Lord lead? Was I really supposed to be there? Should an icky refrigerator have had first priority?

I knew that Jan and Sue would be there. They are identical twins that I'd known only briefly, but had always wanted to know better. I'd been in school with their parents and had heard that the entire family had all been drawn much closer to the Lord because of Sue, who, after two years of bewilderment from undefinable symptoms, had finally been diagnosed as having multiple sclerosis.

But only moments after I walked in, did I know for certain that this is where I was supposed to be. Not so much for my ministering, as for my being ministered to . . . in total merriment.

I don't know if it was when I heard Sue, who was single, exclaiming, "When I saw this handsome doctor, I grabbed Jan's arm and murmured, 'Quick! Tell me what kind of doctor he is so I'll know where to hurt,' " that I decided God wanted me there just to have fun and relax, or if it was when I heard her sharing that "my kidney specialist is such a doll, I think he could take my bladder out and put a tennis shoe in, and I wouldn't object," that maybe I got the picture that the two of us were meant for each other . . . or maybe it was when we were in each other's arms weeping as God met us when we prayed together.

There were only four of us. Peg, myself and these two zany, loving, bubbly twins. They are twenty-three. Jan had been married for two years and was expecting her first baby. Sue found she needed every waking moment of her day to concentrate on just coping . . . she tearfully recounted how she had trouble accepting the fact that, once, she was a busy, vibrant go-getter working for two oral surgeons, and now she walked with a cane, wet her pants on occasion and cried whenever anyone said hello—without even knowing why she cried!

I think we ran the whole gamut of emotions. One moment we were laughing hysterically, and wiping away tears . . . or huddled together in prayer, wiping away tears. I don't know when I've teetered between two tensions as we did that day. Sue has a way of expressing herself hilariously that reminds me of a female Jerry Lewis. (She may not hanker after that description, but it fits!)

The twins told about escapades as children . . . how one blindfolded the other, then said that "there are no more steps now . . . you can walk by yourself," then laughed gleefully while the other one would stumble down the three remaining steps they'd lied about! They giggled as they recalled things that would make their mother say, "Don't tell me any more—I don't want to hear it! I don't want to hear it!"

They'd talk about how Sue and their older sister once told Jan that "you really aren't our sister, you know. Mom and dad found you on a step." And when the one being convinced said, "I don't believe it! How come we all look alike? I'm gonna' go ask mom!" The other two little connivers would stop her and say, "No! Don't do that! Mom always gets sick and cries when people talk to her about it . . . see, she's really sorry she ever got you . . . and the only reason you look like us is 'cuz we live together, and people who live together eat the same food and that makes 'em look alike."

They also told about the unique feature of being twins . . . that when Jan got pregnant, Sue experienced morning sickness for several days . . . and prior to Sue's diagnosis, Jan would get emotionally disturbed and go into deep depressions and have some of the same symptoms. Because she was an identical twin, she then had to be examined to see that she didn't also have the disease. But Jan and Sue wouldn't want all of this to end on a negative note. Sue's faith is strong, and deep in her heart she sees herself as she used to be, believing that this is how she will be again, someday. She is being told that "a cure is only months away," but she said, "When you are twenty-three and in pain, months can drag into years and seem like an eternity. I'm willing to spend every penny I have to find a way . . . God wants me well, and He can touch me at any time, but I know that He understands *my* need to do what *I* can, and use that which is already available . . . I've got *so* much living yet to do! I don't really want the same "me" back that used to be—the "me" that thought that all that was important in life was "whoopin it up" . . . no, I just want the healthy "me" back again—but a "me" that has embraced Christ and doesn't ever want to let go of Him. This whole situation has brought us all closer to the Lord—it's been a valuable experience... but oh, how I long to climb a ladder, paint a room, drive a car...."

And we cried with her. And we all know that God met us there that day. We felt His Spirit, and He heard our cry. I don't really think this chapter is finished yet, but for all intents, we'll say it is for now. I'll go do what I can with the fridge... I'll woo the mice away from the laundry... I'll tidy up the premises like a good housewife should do... but I'll keep you informed of the progress. And when you pass a donation box marked MS... drop something in there, just for Sue. She doesn't relish the view of life from a wheelchair.

57

Sister Nora had come by. We were sitting on the sofa, chatting as enthusiastically as two schoolgirls, forgetting that I am old enough to be her mother. In the Spirit, these distinctions never crop up. And I have never been intimidated by her ecclesiastical habit. (Gene says I have a few ecclesiastical habits of my own!)

As usual, I held her hands as they are always so cold. Her porcelain face looked a little weary, but her voice was so full of comfort. God always seems to send her by when I need a lifting up.

Just before she left, she handed me an envelope and shyly said, "I want to share this with you, but you may use it any way you wish." We hugged and went our separate ways. She, to any number of "people needs" that were always facing her, and I, to my favorite mulling-over place.

The long envelope contained a prayer that she'd penned. My heart was so touched, I want to share it with you.

She wrote:

Dear Jesus, this night I just want to thank you for loving me and for continuing to cover and surround me with that special love which only you

166

can provide. You know that I am not worthy to receive even a little portion of what you have to give me, but you are so great and so wonderful that no matter how terrible I am you still continue to call me your child and heir to all that is to come.

Days seem so long and nights, also. I long for you and beg you daily to come and take me unto yourself. Life is lonely, Lord. You alone know my sufferings and pain. With you it is easier to understand, but it still hurts me to feel this inner-spiritual despair. I would just ask that you would forgive me for all that I have done, and not done to praise you and thank you.

You know our hearts, Lord, and you alone are aware of what is important to us. Give us courage to run to you and drop into your outspread arms. When we fall you will reach down to pick us up. When we look back, you keep telling us to press forward to our goal. Remind us over and over again that you have a plan for our lives. You want us to be yours and to grow in love until we become one with you.

Lord, it is good that we do not have to be alone. You have in your plan brought a great light to shine in our darkness. Each light we see is bright and it will only flicker or die out when we are selfish or unconcerned. I just thank you and praise you so much for showing the light to me through those around me. These small lights have tried to outshine the great darkness which is overpowering me. Hear me and help me. I know that I have failed to be what you have expected. Oh, God—I am so sorry. Those around me have left me in quietness because they don't know what to do.

Fill me with your Spirit that I may give until it hurts . . . until I realize that it is not my eyes or ears or lips, but yours that I am to use. It is so difficult for me to realize that the end is so close and that the time is so short. What can I do? How can it all be done? Guide us, Lord, so that one day we might feel ourselves walking in the cool grass which you have prepared for us.

You tell us that you are the Lord and that there is nothing else to want for. You tell us that when our earthly tent we now live in is taken down . . . when we die and leave these bodies—we will have wonderful new bodies in heaven, homes that will be ours forever more, made for us by yourself and not by any of us. You tell us that to look forward with confidence to our heavenly bodies, realizing that every moment we spend in these earthly bodies is time spent away from you. Why then do we fear? Do we not believe you?

You have given us the free gift. You have sent us salvation. You have sent the one who is to guide us until you come again in glory. I just want to raise you up to everyone around me. I want everyone to know that to see is not enough, but to believe is most important to you.

Give us hope to see that we have a wonderful new relationship with you because of what you have done and suffered for us. Give us each day a foretaste of the things to come.

Help us to understand the massiveness of your plans for us, more fully. Hear us when we pray. We are so blessed, and we thank you for these blessings.

Lord, I am so inadequate and so helpless. I know that if I will run after the likeness of the Holy Spirit I will find peace and joy. Why do I always seek after my own desires and so quickly forget what you have placed before me? Help me, Lord. Hear me always when I fall before you in distress. I open myself to you and beg that I might be pleasing to you. You have told me that nothing can separate us from your love. You have told me that even though worms destroy this body, that still I shall see you. Great God, be our guide.

Sister Nora

I pulled the afghan up around me and burrowed more deeply into the chair. I knew that God was blending our hearts together in a strong bond of love, and I'd shared with her that I wanted to be there when God did His miracle, for I knew that He was going to do one of two things. He was going to miraculously heal her, or He would take her home to be with Him in such triumphal glory that we would hear the angelic hosts singing their praises, even down here on this old sin-encrusted earth where wicked men greet each new day with disregard and indifference.

But either way, she and I were going to wait for His decision with a childlike eager anticipation. No one can boast of tomorrow with any assurance, anyhow . . . we don't know what a day is going to bring forth . . . but when God is in it, it has to be good! So we are filling our days with thoughts of Him, and because our minds are stayed on Him, He is sure to give us peace. He's promised it! And He keeps His promises.

58

In this age of rebellion, inflation, self-seeking, unions, and what not, I don't know if this set of rules that actually existed in an office in 1859 will make you chuckle . . . or hurt.

Listen to this:

Office Rules—1859

1.) Office employees will daily sweep the floors, dust the furniture, shelves, and showcases.

2.) Each day fill lamps, clean chimneys, and trim wicks. Wash windows once a week.

3.) Each clerk will bring in a bucket of water and a scuttle of coal for the day's business.

4.) Make your pens carefully, you may whittle nibs to your individual taste.

5.) This office will be open at 7 A.M. and close at 8 P.M. daily, except on the Sabbath, on which day it will remain closed. Each employee is expected to spend the Sabbath by attending church and contributing liberally to the cause of the Lord.

6.) Men employees will be given an evening off each week for courting purposes, or two evenings a week if they go to church.

7.) After an employee has spent thirteen hours of labor in the office, he should spend the time reading the Bible and other good books while contemplating the glories and the building up of the Kingdom.

8.) Every employee should lay aside from each pay a goodly sum of his earnings for his benefit during his declining years, so that he will not become a burden upon the charity of his betters.

9.) Any employee who smokes Spanish cigars, uses liquor in any form, gets shaved at a barber shop or frequents pool and public halls, will give me good reason to suspect his worth, intention, integrity, and honesty.

10.) The employee who has performed his labors faithfully and without fault for a period of five years in my service and who has been thrifty and attentive to his religious duties, and is looked upon by his fellowmen as a substantial and law-abiding citizen, will be given an increase of five cents per day in his pay, providing a just return in profits from the business permits it.

My husband has these rules on the wall in his plant, but I doubt if too many have ever stopped to read them. There is no signature, or indication as to where these were taken from, but I've a suspicion that maybe Scrooge wrote these up. . . .

59

Many people ask me how I started writing. Usually I reply, "Just one word at a time. I concluded that if I could write a word, I could write a sentence; if I could write a sentence, I could write a paragraph, and if I could write a paragraph, who knows but what maybe I couldn't write a chapter, and so forth. . . ."

But this is how I started writing according to the gospel of Gene: He said, "I think, as I recall, it went something like this. Through various stages of creativity, I heard Char say:

" 'Gene, I think I'm going to write a book, I will need a small portable typewriter and a bi-i-i-ig wastebasket. That's all.'

" 'Gene, I'm just into the book. . . I need a small file and a bigger wastebasket.'

" 'Gene, I'm doing well with the book. Only I need a larger portable typewriter and a small desk.'

" 'Gene, I'm really going great guns . . . only I need a larger file. A special lamp. And I'd like one of those new typewriters—you know, the kind that has the little ball that flips and bobbles, plans menus and practically changes diapers. . . .'

" 'Gene, I need a larger desk . . . now I need a stronger

stand for the new typewriter . . . Gene, it doesn't all fit in the pantry . . . could we add on a room?"

" 'Gene, I need someone to cook for me . . . and to help with the house . . . Gene? Gene? You WHAT! Want to marry the cook? Absurd! We signed a contract! Yes, dear—right away dear . . . I'll cook your favorite meal, dear.' "

60

The gauntness of November is thick around me. The leaves have relinquished their lease on life and lie in sodden heaps, their tattered nerve ends against the earth, longing to cover and protect as God had intended, but nevertheless shuddering as prongs of steel and bamboo forcibly rearrange their meaning in life.

And I, I falteringly but gingerly mince my way toward the mid-century mark of my existence with a quickened heartbeat. Oh, nothing physical—just simply the anticipation I feel at wanting to roll out each day crisply, so I can see what God has dropped into it.

When I say "crisply" and "roll-out" I don't mean as in pie dough, for mine has an exasperating tendency to stick and glob to the accompaniment of grunts and sighs. No, I mean roll out, as in "scroll." Each day is a bit ragged-edged and bumply but parchment fresh and crackly with humor as God brings those across my parchment and we all become "bound up in the bundle of life" together. Oh, my. That doesn't mean bundling, as in the Old New England custom but as in 1 Samuel 25:29.

I've told my kids I rather like being "over the hill" because then I don't have to see what they are doing on the other side

. . . and it's much quieter on my side. Actually, I'm enjoying maturity immensely. The passions of youth have simmered . . . somewhat. At least to the place where you can have meaningful relationships with the opposite sex without creating a wave of trauma with every "hello." Responsibilities are not as heavy as they used to be. And at long last, I can begin to wear clothes that "feel good" instead of because I was deluded into thinking they "looked good." Even my eye doctor chuckled when he saw my choice of new frames. I would have thought the designer would have called them by color but no—they are now being given "names." These were called "Autumn"!

I suppose I'm enjoying maturity the most because I can take the time to develop the richness of life that God intended I should. I heard someone say on the radio that "the only ones who resent old age as they come to the end of their lives are those who have lived a shallow existence, for they are haunted by the nagging suspicion that they'd never really lived, after all."

My mother is now gravely ill, and in a nursing home. Pitifully, she will say to us, "Oh, how did this ever happen?" And realistically, we reply, "Mom, it happened to you one day at a time, and you have kept at it for almost eighty-six years." But she is very incoherent at times, and gets quite verbal so it was necessary that they put someone in the room with her who could put up with her verbosity.

I'm not sure I was quite prepared for their choice. I shuddered when I saw her roommate, Pearl, for the first time. She was ugly, lean, and totally "out of it." She spent all of her time in the locked prison of her body going through arm and hand gyrations from her over-sized highchair that somehow gave you the impression that she was weaving, or spinning. Consequently, we referred to her as the "Spinner" instead of her given name, Pearl.

On Thanksgiving Day, my sister Lauraine and I went together to visit mom, this being mom's first holiday apart from us. Because of mom's senility and misery, she seemed rather demanding. We responded to her "move my pillow—rub my back—get me water—scratch my nose" etc., in love.

Our backs were starting to ache as we hovered over her, and once, while straightening out a kink in mine, I said, "Lauraine! That sound—what is it? I think it's Pearl . . . and I think she's crying!"

Lauraine replied, "No, it couldn't be—I don't think she's capable of tears. . . ." But she moved as quickly as I did to Pearl's side, almost fearfully, as the nurses had warned us, "Stay away from Pearl, or she'll get you in a viselike grip!"

But the sound of those tears and the obedience in our step caused something to happen. As we stepped from mom's bed to her chair, a rush of unadulterated agape love was shed abroad in our hearts for this unlovable wretch. I put my arms around her, and Lauraine began to pat her as we asked her forgiveness for not seeing her as a person. She couldn't answer a word as she hadn't spoken an intelligible word in years, but she seemed to respond and wanted to look deeply into our eyes, with an indescribable hunger for love and affection. I cuddled her head in my arms and began to pray, asking God to speak to her deep within her spirit, assuring her of our love and concern, now that we realized she could even comprehend our presence. Lauraine and I were both crying softly with her, and feeling the presence of the Lord as we gave a drink of cold water to this, surely the very "least of the brethren." After we'd patted and loved her some time, she released her hold on us, looked longingly into our eyes again, then clearly and distinctly whispered, "Than-n-nk you-u-u."

We were nearly beside ourselves with joy! And she had stopped crying.

It became an even greater day of Thanksgiving for us, when we heard that one grateful utterance. And Lauraine and I looked deeply at each other, quietly wondering what shape we will be in, when later years become a reality. We realized how really short life is. And how important it is, to make use of each moment that we have, to allow God to fill each moment with His own pulsating, life-giving energy . . . the same energy that raised Christ from the dead. But are we aware that this same power is ours? I wonder. . . .

61

I think it's hilarious that we grownups, even so-called authentic Christian grownups, still have little games that we play with one another. And not all of them are bad games, really. We have the "dress-up and be neat for the sake of one another," and I personally appreciate that game. There is the "don't say what you really think or they will not think of you as a 'good guy.' " That one may be a bit more dishonest.

But the game I see people playing often, and I'm not sure it's all bad because in this day and age when the art of talking has almost become lost, at least it keeps the communication ball rolling. I'm talking about the game called "can you top this?" You know how it goes. Someone tells something, and you come back with, "Oh, yes—something similar happened to me when I . . ." and without realizing it, you have edged yourself into somewhat of a bit more superior place, because your tidbit has a bit more pizazz than the other fellow's.

Well, the other night, I'll have to admit—I came out feeling pretty smug, as my story couldn't be topped as far as God's dealing miraculously in an almost unheard of situation. In fact, I hadn't thought of the incident for years, but when Steve told about placing a book and his checkbook on top of his car, forgetting it, and driving away only to have them returned to him all muddied and shredded, it really *did* remind me of a thrilling incident in our lives, which is, after all, the reason I write books!

It was thirteen years ago. Gene was in the appliance business then, and had just had a great week-long sale. He had a late Saturday night delivery to make, had just phoned me to say that he would be late and not to wait up for him. I was almost due to have Jamie at the time, and didn't rest well anyhow, so I decided to scrub the kitchen floor while the "runway" was clear with the other five all nestled in bed.

I was sloshing around in soapy water and having a generally good time, secretly wondering if a little slip in the suds might not shorten my waiting period, when Gene appeared through the back door in a visibly shaken condition.

"Char, you can't imagine what I just did. As I was about to get into the truck to make the delivery, I saw that the merchandise wasn't really secure enough, so before I got into the truck, I very foolishly put the bank bag with all the day's receipts in it on top of the bed of the truck, retied the rope of the refrigerator I had to deliver, then got back into the truck and took off . . . I never put the bag in with me. I didn't remember it until I left the customer's house. It really made me sick, but I know that it's done and over with and only God knows where that bag is. I retraced my route, but it's pitch black out there, and I couldn't see a thing."

I wanted to be the understanding wife and make all the right sounds, but I, too, was dismayed when I realized that the bank bag contained probably close to three thousand dollars in checks, cash and contract sales. Most of that money was needed to meet the store overhead and debts we had to pay for merchandise on floor plan.

Gene and I prayed together, and quietly, if somewhat

tearfully on my part, relinquished the money to the Lord. We called one or two others, those we knew to be real prayer warriors, and fell into bed tired, but very much at peace.

The next morning, the church service was very comforting and reassuring. The music touched our hearts, as it had so much to do with trusting God, and giving our all to Him.

As we drove home, our hearts were very refreshed, and we couldn't help giggling with the kids about the sights we were seeing. You see, this was only a few weeks after the Palm Sunday tornado and debris from the storm was still scattered all over. The sight that sent them into gales of laughter was a shredded bra hanging from a tree . . . they were too young to realize how the debris reminded us of the grief, the loss of life others experienced . . . and the additional hopelessness of ever finding the bank bag because of the debris.

We were all humming one of the choruses we'd heard at church, when suddenly Gene slammed on the brakes and after a careful glance backwards, began to back up the car.

"Gene, I'm eager to get to the hospital, but not with whiplash . . . whatever are you doing?"

"I don't know for sure, but. . . ."

He didn't bother to finish his sentence. He just walked over to the ditch beside the highway, stepped gingerly through cans, scattered clothing, broken limbs and trivia . . . and picked up the missing bank bag. I could hardly believe my eyes! (Lu says, "Why are we Christians always saying I could hardly believe it? No wonder we don't see too many miracles!")

Needless to say, it was a time of real rejoicing in the car. The Lord knew of our attachment and need of money when He used the illustration of the woman who'd lost the coin, and her great concern. Gene got into the car, gave us all a hug and commented, "We were all singing, and I felt so good

. . . when I saw a glint of sun hit just the metal tip end of the zipper . . . that was all I saw, but I thought it was worth taking a closer look . . . wow, I am so grateful!" And we all began to praise and thank the Lord . . . what a great thing for my children to witness.

62

Every Christian should be "good news" going someplace to happen. Tomorrow night, Lord willing, I'll be speaking in front of the "Singles for Christ" in the area at a local church. I've already gotten the scuttlebutt that some of them are a bit piqued to think that a "married person" would have anything to say that would help a "single" to cope better with life. Comments like that don't exactly pave my way with palm branches before I enter, but then, I'd never sit well on a donkey, either.

Well, hopefully, I must first put them at ease. How I thank God for this treasured sense of humor that gets me absolutely drunk in the Spirit at given intervals. Like it or not, we still have need of ice-breakers. "Barrier crashers" would be a more realistic name for them. But we are all so full of mistrust—insecurities, inferiorities, and inadequacies. They will need to know, right off the bat, that I am one *with* them . . . not above them, or below them. And God's message is not divided—one message for marrieds, and another for singles . . . but that He has come so that they might have life, and more abundantly.

I may even introduce myself as "Church of Messiah's Mother Inferior." And ever so gently, I am believing that God will move me into a discourse of thoughts, gleanings and insights that will help them to see themselves not so much as "single" versus "married" but as persons, either believing, or unbelieving, and each one deposited into a particular set of circumstances that have been custom-made for that particular moment in time just for them, permitted by a God who really is the Blessed Controller of all things.

Perhaps I will share with them about a young girl of thirty who felt there could be no happiness in her life unless she was married. How my heart aches for those who continually think "I could be happy if. . . ." Life, and trials, and Christian growth have taught me that any time your happiness depends upon an outward circumstance being changed, or on the addition of one more person into your life, then your happiness is never going to be stable. Happiness, to be attained, must be founded upon a solid "rock" . . . a relationship that sinks its roots right into the heart of God, to be fed and nourished straight from that rock that is higher than I. A foundation, yet above and surrounding—pervading and living. The Word tells us that He has lavished us with the riches of God's grace. Think of that for a moment! *Lavished*—dipped and sozzled and dripping with the riches, the wealth, the glories of His grace; that available ability that makes us know that we are complete in Him and have total access *to* Him! Oh, my word—I think I'm getting a bit drunk already, and goodness knows—I get into so much trouble sober, I can't afford to be drunk—unless, of course, it is drunk in the Spirit. Now where was I—oh, yes. I was wanting to be "good news" going someplace to happen. But for the moment, I'd better be good wife going someplace to housekeep.

63

Sometimes, I just want to grab people by the lapel and shout, "Hey! I know there is a person deep inside of me and I know there is one inside of you! Now come out, so I can know you . . . do you hear?" But instead, I smile demurely, and patiently listen to "Hello—how are you? Oh, I'm fine . . . yes, the weather is lovely—no, I've lived here all my life," and secretly, I'm nursing an ache that comes from the realization that our guardedness is part of the Fall; our reluctance to share on a deep meaningful level stems from our inability to share our innermost beings, because of our lack of trust. Truly, our sins have separated us from God and from one another.

But there is hope in Christ Jesus! I see it happening all around me . . . as people are giving God access to their hearts, they are timidly beginning to share their hurts and hearts with one another. The closer we draw to Him, the closer we will draw to one another. "If we walk in the light, as he is in the light, we have fellowship one with another, and the blood of Jesus Christ his Son cleanseth us from all sin" (1 John 1:7). Our greatest work, then, is to simply expose ourselves to that light. God does the rest!

64

I was so very cross last night. Somehow, counselors are never to get cross, never have problems, never make mistakes, are always to be strong, always cheerful . . . and I ask myself, "Who made these rules, anyhow? God didn't. He has promised to love me with as deep a love in the midst of my humanity as He does in the depths of any so-called spirituality."

But you may be muttering to yourself, "What has she got to be cross about?" Well, for one thing, I'm bearing a precious treasure around in a vessel of clay and all I seem to be aware of is the dust in my mouth. But that's not the reason for my crossness—in fact, that is the very hope of my deliverance.

My biggest hassle at this moment is the fact that it is December 23 and the pressure of tradition, that deadly, choking but-we've-always-done-it-this-way torment is stifling me again. That leering voice just over my shoulder screaming, "This year, you're not going to make it . . . I'll squeeze the very life out of you with all this pressure and you'll be a limp, unspiritual clod, you just wait and see!"

But, do you know, I've never missed a Christmas in my almost thirty years of marriage? Somehow, miraculously, there have always been presents under the tree, cookies in the jar, ornaments dangling where they should be dangling, things neatly in place (granted, only *moments* before the guests arrive!), and so, I must psych myself into believing that yes, perhaps again this year, Christmas might just fade into the past as it has for so many years.

Please don't misunderstand me—I love the family togetherness of Christmas. I love the sharing times, the little special touches. I just don't like the pressure that manages to make me feel cross. So the problem is within me, not with Christmas.

But the very fact that the pressure can affect me, is my greatest reason for rejoicing at Christmas, for that bit of weakness is a part of the manger scene in my own heart. The awe of Christmas still goes on within, for the Christ child grows daily within me, surrounded by the filth and degradation of my heart, the impatience, the lusting, the envying, the wanting to hurt others if they've hurt me. . . it's all there. How graciously He remains steadfastly in my innermost being, in spite of what surrounds Him.

Well, perhaps the crossness worked a repentance in my heart—at any rate, I picked up the beloved story again, and read it carefully and found myself weeping when I read about the baby boys being killed, for had I lived there and been one of those daughters of Rachel, my little Thad would have been killed! What sorrow was attached to Christ's being born. And afresh, I realized the hauntingness of reproduction. That children are given, and then they have children, and your life is never the same again because of that quiet hovering cloud that rests behind the heart of every woman—the knowing that each child could be recalled to his Maker at any given moment.

Another thing that struck me as I read the old familiar story was the absolute "headship" that God granted to Joseph, and Mary's total acceptance that God had said it. She must have had complete faith that God would speak to her through her husband, for God told Joseph (in a dream) to get up and take the child and his mother into Egypt. So he did it—he got up, took the child, and Mary didn't give him any hassle, didn't tell him they should consult the elders first, didn't come back with "if God wanted us to do that He'd speak it to my heart, too," didn't fuss because she'd not been given time to do the laundry, she just simply submitted, "as unto the Lord."

Twice again, we see where Joseph's dream life caused more uprooting in the lives of young Jesus and patient Mary, but her trust was in God, and she believed that God would give her direction through her husband. How far from that we have gotten!

Yes, we are in the twentieth century, now. And it's Christmas. I've been busy baking things that are loaded with sugar, will give us all heartburn, substituting junk foods and quickie meals to "buy time" to bake, gift-wrap, and decorate, growling at the neighbor kids to "stay out"—because it's Christmas, you see—a time to be merry—y'see.

65

By the stack of papers in my folder, the disorganized look to my closets, and the gentle prod from my publisher, I've the sneaky suspicion that I'm nearing the end of this book. When drawers start bulging and cobwebs drape the oven, I'll know it's definitely time to draw all this to a close.

But I've never had any lessons in book ending—or sentence finishing. And when I go into eternity, I know I'll have both fists full of unfinished sentences . . . I even said once, to my pastor, "Lu, when we get to heaven can we finish all the sentences we started down here? Will you take the time to talk with me?"

He grinned and sighed, "Well, I would Char . . . but then it wouldn't be heaven any more." I roared, but I knew what he was trying to say, from a weary pastor's frame of reference.

Well, life is like a manuscript. When it is finished, then it is really just beginning . . . if you've permitted Christ to have access to your heart, your thoughts, your will, that is.

Let me share a portion of a beautiful little book, *Under His Wings* by O. Hallesby. It is taken from a chapter titled "Martha and Mary," and he is bringing out the wisdom of Mary, for having chosen "the good part, which shall not be taken away from her."

I quote: "Naturally you love your home and take care of it as well and make it as cozy as you can. But some day you will have to part with it, without further notice. A casket will transport you away from it. And others will move in, only after an extra good housecleaning. They desire to obliterate thoroughly every trace of you.

"You love the flowers in your garden and care for them lovingly and tenderly. Oftentimes they gladden your heart both by their beauty and their fragrance. But some day they will render you their last service: they will deck your casket. And then wither upon your grave.

"You have money. And you love your money, whether you have much or little. But some day it, too, will be taken from you. Others will divide it among themselves. Your bank account will be transferred to other names.

"Your abilities are in a special sense your own. And perhaps you have great ability, both physical and mental. But some day it, too, will be gone. You will not even be able to lift your hand to brush a fly from your face.

"Perhaps you are a clear thinker and have a keen intellect. But some day you will lose your consciousness also and thereby the use of your faculties.

"You have loved ones, who love you and who are kind to you. And you are grateful for their love.

"But some day these tender ties, too, will be severed . . . through death's portal you must pass alone. . . ."

Dear ones, I'm not trying to bring the curtain down on the last act of this book with some kind of Shakespearean flair . . . . I'm merely pointing out the fact that life, although very much worth the living, still must come to an end. We will stand before almighty God, and He will judge us according to what we have done in the body, but the basis for that judging

189

will be, "What have you done with my Son, Jesus? Have you believed on Him, whom I've sent?"

If you have given this Jesus access to your heart, then you will never have to stand before an angry God, for Jesus paid the full price for your redemption when He died on that cross two thousand years ago. Houses, lands, titles, works . . . nothing will matter at that last day, except your relationship to Jesus Christ. This relationship is that "good part, which shall not be taken away."

Consider Him . . . the wonderful provision that God has made so that we might forever be with Him in eternity. And I really want you there, my friend. Eternity won't be the same without you . . . God bless you all, from this handmaiden of the Lord.

For free information on how to receive
the international magazine

LOGOS JOURNAL

also Book Catalog

Write: Information - LOGOS JOURNAL CATALOG
Box 191
Plainfield, NJ 07061